BestMasters

Mit **„BestMasters"** zeichnet Springer die besten Masterarbeiten aus, die an renommierten Hochschulen in Deutschland, Österreich und der Schweiz entstanden sind. Die mit Höchstnote ausgezeichneten Arbeiten wurden durch Gutachter zur Veröffentlichung empfohlen und behandeln aktuelle Themen aus unterschiedlichen Fachgebieten der Naturwissenschaften, Psychologie, Sozialwissenschaften, Technik und Wirtschaftswissenschaften. Die Reihe wendet sich an Praktiker und Wissenschaftler gleichermaßen und soll insbesondere auch Nachwuchswissenschaftlern Orientierung geben.

Springer awards **"BestMasters"** to the best master's theses which have been completed at renowned Universities in Germany, Austria, and Switzerland. The studies received highest marks and were recommended for publication by supervisors. They address current issues from various fields of research in natural sciences, psychology, social sciences, technology, and economics. The series addresses practitioners as well as scientists and, in particular, offers guidance for early stage researchers.

Karen Ayu Stiller

Securing Peer-to-Peer Identities in IoT Systems Using Blockchain and Multi-Agent Systems with an Outlook on M2M Payment Applications

Springer Gabler

Karen Ayu Stiller
Management
Frankfurt School of Finance &
Management
Frankfurt am Main, Germany

ISSN 2625-3577 ISSN 2625-3615 (electronic)
BestMasters
ISBN 978-3-658-51519-5 ISBN 978-3-658-51520-1 (eBook)
https://doi.org/10.1007/978-3-658-51520-1

This Springer Gabler imprint is published by the registered company Springer Fachmedien Wiesbaden GmbH, part of Springer Nature.
The registered company address is: Abraham-Lincoln-Str. 46, 65189 Wiesbaden, Germany

Acknowledgement

I would like to thank my supervisor Prof. Dr. Kai Spohrer for the support and insightful direction, which helped me begin this research with better purpose and focus and I would like to extend my gratitude to my second supervisor Prof. Dr. Christoph Kreiterling for the thoughtful advice and encouragement, which provided both clarity and motivation. Once again, to my parents, Ria Pertiwi-Stiller and Dr. Dietrich Franz Richard Stiller and my little brother Carl Erik Constantin Stiller I am incredibly grateful, for their support and love. And to my cats Honzi, Urlina, Fröstelchen and Marshmallow, your presence provided comfort during the long hours of research and writing. Thank you.

Contents

1 Introduction 1
1.1 Machine-to-Machine Economy 1
1.2 Security Threats in Machine-To-Machine 2
1.3 Purpose of the Thesis 2
1.4 Thesis Structure 3

2 Literature Review 5
2.1 Internet of Things 5
2.1.1 Internet of Things Architecture 6
2.1.2 Mobile Ad hoc NETworks 6
2.1.3 Machine-To-Machine 7
2.1.4 Possible Threats 8
2.1.5 Countermeasures 9
2.2 Multi-Agent Systems 9
2.3 Blockchain 10
2.3.1 Decentralized Identifiers 10
2.3.2 Self Sovereign Identities 11
2.3.3 Smart Contracts 11
2.4 Sybil Attacks 11
2.4.1 Sybil Attack Defences 13
2.5 Related Work 14
2.5.1 Local, Collaborative and Mobility Detection 15
2.5.2 Trust Modelling 16
2.5.3 Identity Anchoring and Trust Ledger Design 17

2.5.4 Consensus-Level Robustness 19
2.5.5 Trustless and Distributed Detection Signals 19
2.5.6 Power Scaling and Active Sybil Attacks 21
2.5.7 Simulation Frameworks 21

3 Research Design 23
3.1 Design Science Stages 24

4 Methodology 27
4.1 Objectives 27
4.2 Threat Model and Attack Scenarios 28
4.3 Model Structure 28
4.3.1 Algorithmic Components 30
4.4 Metrics 31
4.5 Scope and Limitations 32

5 Implementation 33
5.1 Simulated Environment 33
5.2 Simulation Architecture 35
5.2.1 Layer 1 36
5.2.2 Layer 2 41
5.2.3 Layer 3 44
5.2.4 Layer 4 45
5.2.5 Layer 5 47
5.3 Metrics Collection 50

6 Results and Analysis 55
6.1 Experimental Setup 55
6.2 Detection Performance 57
6.2.1 Layer 1 57
6.2.2 Layer 2 58
6.2.3 Layer 3 59
6.2.4 Comparison between Layers 60
6.3 Economic Impact 64

7 Discussion 67
7.1 Contribution 69
7.2 Limitations 71
7.2.1 Future Work 72

8 Conclusion 75

Bibliography 77

Abbreviations

AUC	Area Under Curve
BFT	Byzantine Fault Tolerance
BNL	Boneh-Lynn-Shacham
DAG	Directed Acyclic Graphs
DHT	Distributed Hash Tables
DID	Decentralized Identifier
ETX	Expected Transmission Count
FPR	False Positive Ratio
IDS	Intrusion Detection System
IoT	Internet of Things
M2M	Machine-To-Machine
MANET	Mobile ad hoc Network
MAS	Multi-Agent System
P2P	Peer-To-Peer
PGFA	Probabilistic Generating Function Analysis
PSO	Particle Swarm Optimization
ROC	Receiver Operating Characteristic
RSSI	Received Signal Strength Indicator
RSU	Road Side Unit
RTT	Round-Trip Time
SF-MRTS	Sybil-Free Metric-based Routing Protocol Trustworthiness Scheme
SSI	Self-Sovereign Identity
TDOA	Time Difference of Arrival
TPR	True Positive Ratio
TTC	Trust and Transactions Chain
VANET	Vehicular ad hoc network
WSN	wireless sensor networks

List of Figures

Fig. 2.1 Architecture adapted from Al-Fuqaha et al. (2015) and Yang et al. (2017). (© 2015 IEEE. © 2017 IEEE. Reprinted with permission) ... 7
Fig. 2.2 Schematic diagram of network nodes' locations, adapted from Dong et al. (2022). Licensed under CC BY 4.0 ... 12
Fig. 2.3 An example of deploying nodes in the first execution round of the algorithm from Jamshidi et al. (2017). (© 2016 Elsevier. Reprinted with permission) ... 16
Fig. 2.4 Example of the block creation process when agents A and B have participated in a transaction, adapted from Otte, de Vos & Pouwelse (2020). (© 2017 Elsevier. Reprinted with permission) ... 18
Fig. 2.5 Illustration of (a) traditional blockchain, (b) IOTA Tangle, and (c) two-layer ISCP architecture where two possible chains anchored to different Table nodes are highlighted. (Adapted from Keramat, Queralta & Westerlund (2023). Licensed under CC BY 4.0) ... 20
Fig. 3.1 Framework for Evaluation in Design Science with evaluation strategies from Venable et al., (2016). Licensed under CC BY 4.0. ... 24
Fig. 6.1 Comparison of ROC curves ... 61
Fig. 6.2 Comparison of TPR for different S-values ... 62
Fig. 6.3 Comparison of AUC for different S-values ... 63
Fig. 7.1 Comparison of TPR across N ... 69
Fig. 7.2 Comparison of ROC curves ... 70

List of Tables

Table 2.1 Overview of related work 22
Table 5.2 Simulation Architecture 35
Table 5.2 Notations used in the equations 41
Table 6.1 Experimental Parameters 55
Table 6.2 Simulation Architecture 56
Table 6.3 Performance under base parameters 57

Introduction

1

With the growth of the 5G infrastructure and the advancements in distributed ledgers, Internet of Things (IoT) devices are increasingly capable of autonomous interactions. The market size of Machine-To-Machine (M2M) is valued at USD 23.62 billion in 2023 and is expected to reach USD 35.40 billion by 2032 (SNS Insider, 2025) and M2M payments are following, with Commerzbank AG starting their pilot in 2019 (Commerzbank AG, 2019).

As this area continues to grow, it will be important to be able to detect and prevent attacks. Given the importance of identity and the similarities to Peer-To-Peer (P2P), Sybil attacks, a known threat in IoT-Networks, will be especially important to avoid (Bochem & Leiding, 2021).

1.1 Machine-to-Machine Economy

The idea behind the Machine-To-Machine Economy is that smart machines are communicating autonomously and exchanging information for economic purposes. The concept of the economy of things is thought to have machines that are able to issue invoices and make payments among themselves without human intervention.

K. A. Stiller, *Securing Peer-to-Peer Identities in IoT Systems Using Blockchain and Multi-Agent Systems with an Outlook on M2M Payment Applications*, BestMasters, https://doi.org/10.1007/978-3-658-51520-1_1

This vision has driven significant research into the integration of cryptocurrencies with consumer and industrial IoT. By enabling devices to perform microtransactions, researchers aim to create a decentralized financial ecosystem for machines. Given the anticipated volume of transactions, scalability and low fees will be needed to ensure operational feasibility and economic viability (Pocher & Zichichi, 2022).

Not only is Commerzbank working on pilots, but also Mastercard is trying to open up more possibilities in micro-payments for Pay-Per-Use and M2M scenarios with their GO-NET payment platform (Mastercard, 2021).

1.2 Security Threats in Machine-To-Machine

The decentralized peer-to-peer architecture of M2M makes it particularly vulnerable to Sybil attacks, where malicious entities simulate multiple identities to exploit the network. This vulnerability is especially serious in the context of automated payments, where communication occurs without human oversight.

With lack of oversight, malicious interactions may not be detected immediately, potentially disturbing a system's integrity and financial security. Furthermore, as machines increasingly interact with and influence the physical world, there is a great risk of safety. Ensuring robust data security, verifying data sources, and restricting access to authorized parties will be important; therefore, secure transmission protocols must be in place to prevent tampering and interception (Pradhan & Tun, 2022).

1.3 Purpose of the Thesis

The purpose of this study is to create a proof of concept to detect and prevent Sybil attacks in M2M networks. This proof-of-concept will be based on existing IoT research that works to detect and prevent Sybil attacks. The goal is to create an improved approach, based on known advantages and limitations, that is scalable for micro-transactions and computationally feasible for low-powered IoT devices.

1.4 Thesis Structure

The thesis begins with a theoretical background of the used technologies and continues with related work, on which the methodology will be based. The methodology, using the framework of design science will explain the process of building the simulation, enhancing it using findings from other research and then showcasing the results. These will be compared and discussed. Lastly in the conclusion, the thesis summarizes the findings while discussing limitations and possible future work.

2 Literature Review

This literature review offers a theoretical basis on the technology used in this thesis and the nature of Sybil attacks, followed by an introduction to relevant work on earlier strategies used to detect and prevent Sybil attacks.

2.1 Internet of Things

In 1999, the Internet of Things (IoT) was first described as a system that would allow physically recognizable things to be digitally represented and connected in a manner similar to the internet. This signalled a change from human-centric networks, where information is generated and shared by hand, to a model where data is generated and shared by devices on their own. Almost all of the data available online had been manually recorded, typed, or scanned. These are all processes that were constrained by human accuracy, time and attention. The drawbacks of depending only on human-created information and the requirement for machines to autonomously perceive and interpret the physical world are becoming increasingly visible. IoT addresses this by enabling computers to gather data directly from the environment using technologies such as RFID and sensors. This allows for continuous, automated observations and analysis of physical systems, facilitating real-time decision-making and operational efficiency (Ashton, 2009).

IoT has developed into a large network of networked items that can share resources, organize and react to changes in their surroundings (Madakam, Ramaswamy & Tripathi, 2015). This transformation has been driven by advancements in sensor and actuator networks, tracking and identification technologies,

K. A. Stiller, *Securing Peer-to-Peer Identities in IoT Systems Using Blockchain and Multi-Agent Systems with an Outlook on M2M Payment Applications*, BestMasters, https://doi.org/10.1007/978-3-658-51520-1_2

and enhanced communication protocols that enable distributed intelligence among smart objects. IoT now extends beyond basic connectivity, supporting seamless communication anytime, anywhere and across diverse media. Concepts such as Web Squared, which integrate online technologies with sensing capabilities, further expand the potential of the internet (Atzori, Iera & Morabito, 2010).

2.1.1 Internet of Things Architecture

To understand the architecture of the Internet of Things, many foundational models begin with a three-layer framework including perception, network and application layers. Al-Fuqaha et al. (2015) describe this model in detail. The perception layer gathers data via sensors, the network layer transmits the gathered data and the application layer provides services to end users. However, as IoT systems have evolved, newer models introduce additional layers to reflect the complexity of modern deployments. One such addition is the transportation layer with security mechanisms, which ensures reliable and secure data transmission across applications on the application layer. This layer plays an important role in managing communication between devices and cloud platforms, especially in latency-sensitive and safety-critical applications. While the standard four-layer IoT architecture includes perception, network, transportation and application layers, the transportation layer often incorporates cloud computing platforms in other papers (Fig. 2.1).

2.1.2 Mobile Ad hoc NETworks

Mobile Ad hoc Networks (MANET) are constructed of a set of heterogenous devices equipped with wireless communication capabilities. The devices are completely autonomous without a central entity running the network. Because there is no central routing entity, each device needs to be able to route and forward received packets. The network is characterized by dynamic topology with multihop communications. The links between nodes of the network might disappear or appear based on the mobility of the device. Multi-hop networks require higher security standards, because the communication may be attacked at multiple nodes in the networks (Ahmed & Khalifa, 2017).

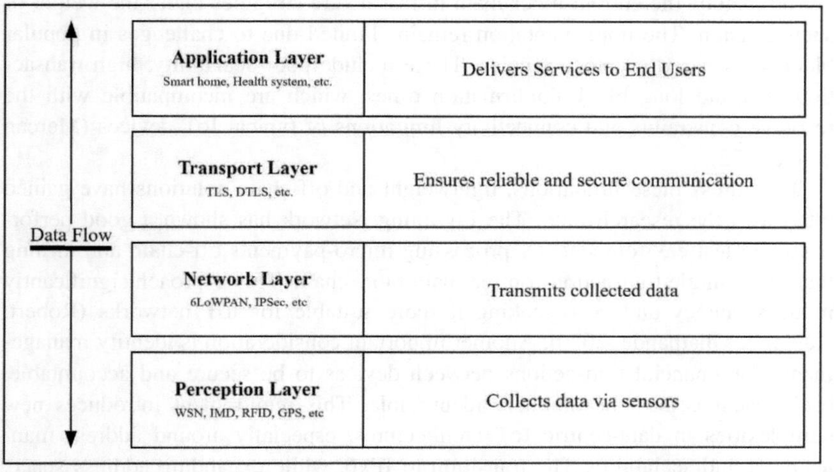

Fig. 2.1 Architecture adapted from Al-Fuqaha et al. (2015) and Yang et al. (2017). (© 2015 IEEE. © 2017 IEEE. Reprinted with permission)

2.1.3 Machine-To-Machine

The term Machine-To-Machine (M2M) is used to describe computers with processors, smart sensors, actuators and mobile devices to communicate and make decisions without human intervention or oversight (Watson et al., 2004). With the incoming 6G Networks, M2M communication might benefit from increased reliability, low latency and higher bandwidth (Rojek et al., 2024). By combining IoT and Blockchain technology, smart machines could process data in automated and transparent ways due to the verifiable, transparent and immutable way of recording their data. The machines can interact with the environment and make self executed decisions through smart contracts. The machines would ideally eliminate agency, coordination cost and possibly lead to highly distributed enterprises with reduced or no management (Mourouzis et al., 2022).

M2M payments represent a promising, currently still largely conceptual part of autonomous digital economies. Despite the conceptual appeal of a decentralized, machine-driven economy, enabling real-time financial exchanges between IoT devices, especially in the form of micro-transactions remains with technical limitations. Micro-transactions are a suitable mechanism for devices to autonomously settle small payments for data, energy use or shared functionality.

Unfortunately, the current blockchain infrastructure struggles under the weight of such a vision. The implementation remains limited due to challenges in popular blockchain based cryptocurrencies. These include poor scalability, high transaction fees and long block confirmation times, which are incompatible with the resource constraints and connectivity limitations of typical IoT devices (Mercan et al., 2022).

To address these limitations, lightweight and off-chain solutions have gained interest in the research field. The Lightning Network has shown a good performance in test environments by processing micro-payments off-chain and turning them into single transactions on the main blockchain. This approach significantly reduces latency and cost, making it more suitable for IoT networks (Robert, Kubler & Ghatpande, 2020). Another important consideration is identity management. For financial transactions between devices to be secure and accountable, each machine must be uniquely identifiable. This requirement introduces new complexities in data-centric IoT architectures, especially around address management and scalability. The transition to IPv6, while expanding address space, also increases pressure on limited storage on constrained IoT devices (Mercan & Akkaya, 2021).

2.1.4 Possible Threats

As in many other sectors, security in IoT networks remains a concern, given its widespread adoption and the multitude of attack vectors it presents. As IoT devices spread across consumer, industrial and infrastructural domains, their exposure to malicious activity increases proportionally. A study by Khan and Salah (2018) has categorized IoT security threats into three tiers, being low-level, intermediate, which include transport-layer vulnerabilities, and high-level threats. It showcases a wide range of attacks, ranging from spoofing and sleep deprivation to denial-of-service, buffer reservation, replay, duplication, sinkhole, wormhole and Sybil attacks. The Sybil attacks, while classified as intermediate-level, carry far-reaching implications. They can lead to privacy breaches, spamming, unreliable broadcasts and even Byzantine faults (Khan & Salah, 2018). However, the relevance of Sybil attacks intensifies in the context of M2M payments, where peer-to-peer connections and identity verification play a big role. In such autonomous financial exchanges, the integrity of each device's identity becomes critical, not only for accountability, but also for ensuring secure and trustworthy transactions for the whole system.

In general, M2M communication introduces unique vulnerabilities within the IoT landscape. Unlike human interactions, machine exchanges often occur without oversight, making it harder to detect malicious behaviour in real time. Additionally, with the integration of IoT devices into everyday life, ranging from smart infrastructure and vehicles to industrial automation, cybersecurity moves from a more digital concern into a tangible, physical threat. These devices now play bigger roles in regulating real-world processes and their compromise can result in operational failures (Pradhan & Tun, 2022). Still, the foundational architectures supporting IoT and M2M communication stay structurally weak. Encryption is important, but difficult to implement consistently across resource-constrained IoT devices. Data ownership tends to be fleeting and the complexity of securing the infrastructure raises serious doubts about the reliability of transaction processing (Jamil et al., 2021).

2.1.5 Countermeasures

Recent research has explored the use of blockchain and multi-agent systems to enhance intrusion detection in IoT environments. Multi-agent systems offer decentralized task management and adaptability to complex IoT architectures by eliminating reliance on centralized nodes, thereby reducing possibility of single point failures. Blockchain introduces trust, transparency and tamper-resistance into the system's data handling and deep learning techniques have shown potential in identifying transport-layer attacks. Positioning intrusion detection systems at strategic points across the IoT architecture allows for comprehensive monitoring across layers. However, the complexity and computational demands of these integrated systems result in high resource consumption, which many IoT networks, especially the ones with constrained nodes, struggle to support (Liang et al., 2020).

2.2 Multi-Agent Systems

Multi-Agent Systems (MAS) consist of autonomous agents that collaborate to solve tasks within their environment. Each agent can sense relevant parameters, make decisions based on their assigned tasks and act accordingly, enabling decentralized problem-solving and adaptability (Dorri, Kanhere & Jurdak, 2018). MAS have been applied to intrusion detection and prevention, often in combination with techniques such as reputation systems, auctions and fuzzy logic. Anomaly-based

MAS approaches are especially common and often integrated with computational intelligence, resulting in distributed intelligence across the network. These MAS-driven systems have shown potential to improve detection accuracy and reduce false alarm rates (Shamshirband et al., 2013). Additionally, according to Dorri, Kanhere & Jurdak (2018), MAS can improve IoT security by enabling distributed intrusion detection systems that are adaptive, scalable, and responsive to evolving attack patterns. Agents perform local analysis and collaborate through trust models to minimize false alarms, while maintaining real-time response capabilities. This decentralized structure reduces pressure on centralized systems and adds resilience to single points of failure.

2.3 Blockchain

Blockchains, a subset of distributed ledger technologies, function as a decentralized database composed of immutable blocks that store transaction data. Each block is cryptographically linked to the previous one, ensuring tamper resistance and transparency across the network (Nakamoto, 2008). Permissionless blockchains like Bitcoin and Ethereum allow wide participation and rely on decentralized consensus mechanisms such as Proof-of-Work or Proof-of-Stake. These systems emphasize openness, privacy and strong decentralization. Permissioned blockchains, on the other hand, require identity registration and typically operate without resource-intensive consensus protocols (Ghiro et al., 2021). The downfall of thee permissioned blockchains is their reliance on a central entity, introducing a single point of failure.

2.3.1 Decentralized Identifiers

Decentralized Identifiers (DIDs) are a solution to the limitations of traditional identity systems. Unlike centralized identifiers governed by third-party authorities, DIDs are created and managed by the user and registered on distributed ledgers, which are a type of distributed database. This allows individuals, organizations or devices to authenticate themselves in a secure way. Each DID links to a corresponding document containing the public keys and metadata necessary for verification of the device, enabling trusted communication between parties (Reed et al., 2022). In IoT networks and digital ecosystems where interoperability and resilience are important, DIDs provide a scalable identity foundation that can adapt to evolving demands, opening up many possibilities (Garzon, Yildiz & Küpper, 2022).

2.3.2 Self Sovereign Identities

Complementing this approach are Self-Sovereign Identities (SSI). With SSI frameworks, users are no longer passive entities in the identity exchange process and actively generate, control and share their digital credentials according to their own policies. These credentials are typically issued by trusted sources like educational institutions, government bodies or employers. This not only safeguards personal data, but also builds trust, because the verification of credentials is handled cryptographically without revealing sensitive information. Therefore, the identity of a user, process or device gets verified, without losing privacy (Dempsey et al., 2011).

2.3.3 Smart Contracts

Smart contracts are self-executing pieces of code that are executed in a decentralized context. They are machine-readable and run directly on the blockchain, providing essential components of larger application programs. Smart contracts are event-driven, which means that they respond to predefined triggers or situations. Once they are activated, they act independently without the need for continual supervision and their decentralized nature provides transparency, resilience and trust (Szabo, 1997).

2.4 Sybil Attacks

The Sybil attacks were first introduced in the paper *The Sybil Attack in Mobile Ad Hoc Networks* by John Douceur in 2002. The Sybil attackers are defined as nodes presenting itself to the network as multiple nodes. These nodes then gain more power in voting or consensus based distribution systems, effectively influencing the outcome of the networks computations.

Sybil attacks in IoT environments are broadly categorized into three distinct types by Zhang et al. (2014). The first involves attackers with limited social connections, commonly observed in sensing and social domains, where minimal interaction is enough to disrupt trust mechanisms. The second type describes

Sybil entities with extensive social links that mimic real users, making them especially effective in social network-based systems. The third category includes mobile-based Sybil attackers, which operate within mobile networks and exploit mobility to evade detection and amplify their influence. Active Sybil attacks pose even greater challenges to network integrity. In these attacks, malicious nodes respond with semantically correct, but intentionally false data, effectively deceiving the system lookup processes, like ones used in Distributed Hash Tables (DHTs). These Sybil nodes are strategically placed to remain below detection thresholds and to exploit early termination mechanisms in content discovery protocols (Netto, Cholez & Ignat, 2025).

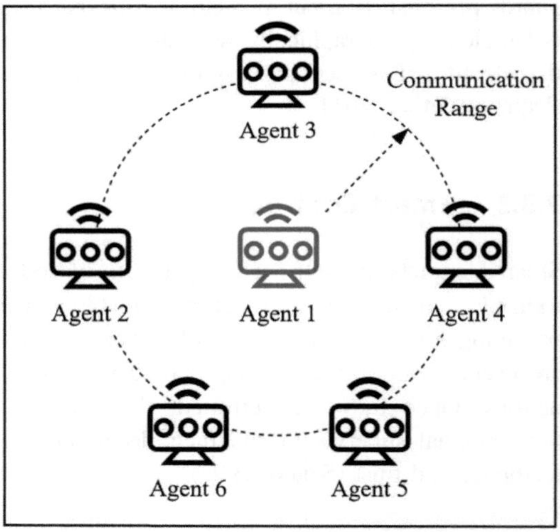

Fig. 2.2 Schematic diagram of network nodes' locations, adapted from Dong et al. (2022). Licensed under CC BY 4.0

Sybil attacks can come in the form of power scaling. Power scaling attacks happen when attackers systematically escalate the influence of compromised nodes by amplifying their capacity, either through increased bandwidth, computational power or battery manipulation. This makes malicious nodes appear disproportionately more trustworthy and reliable compared to their legitimate counterparts. These attacks are especially dangerous in resource-constrained IoT settings, where most devices operate on minimal power and computational capacity. Attackers could exploit power-aware routing protocols by ensuring their Sybil nodes consistently advertise optimal energy levels. Hereby increasing the likelihood of being selected for communication tasks. By simulating high availability, these nodes can dominate critical decision-making flows in distributed systems. Combined with techniques like false data injection, power scaling further skews network topology and trust distribution. What makes this hybrid threat especially strong is its ability to camouflage malicious behaviour behind performance metrics. Unlike traditional Sybil detection mechanisms that rely on link analysis or identity verification, power scaling requires deeper inspection of energy patterns, behavioural consistency and cross-node validation.

2.4.1 Sybil Attack Defences

To detect the three mentioned categories of Sybil attacks in IoT networks, several detection strategies have been created. Social graph-based detection uses trust relationships and network topology to identify anomalous nodes. They are effective against Sybil entities with less social links, as they rely on the limited number of attack edges, but their effectiveness decreases when attackers forge several social connections, blurring the distinction between genuine and malicious nodes.

Behaviour-classification-based detection focuses on user activity patterns, for example clickstream behaviour and applies machine learning algorithms to classify users. This approach works for identifying Sybil nodes that mimic real user behaviour but still exhibit subtle anomalies. Nonetheless, this detection mechanism requires large labelled datasets and supervised learning, leading to high training costs. Additionally, as attackers improve their mimicry, the reliability of behaviour-based models may decline over time. This would introduce the need for re-training the modes, further increasing the training costs.

Lastly, mobile Sybil detection uses mobility analysis, location tracking and cryptographic tokens to differentiate between legitimate and malicious entities. By matching mobility patterns within friend and foe communities, this method works best in mobile environments. However, it introduces privacy concerns due to the collection of sensitive location and contact data and suffers from high computational overhead because of the cryptographic operations and decentralized identity management (Zhang et al., 2014).

Building on these detection strategies, a broader survey of Sybil countermeasures in IoT-based wireless sensor networks (WSNs) was done by Arshad et al. (2021). The survey categorizes defences into five main groups. It describes encryption-based, trust-based, Received Signal Strength Indicator-based (RSSI), artificial intelligence-driven and hybrid approaches. Hybrid approaches often combine ranking algorithms, multi-kernel learning, rule-based logic and encryption schemes, even though the exact classification of these subtypes is different across studies. Each category offers different advantages and limitations. RSSI and trust-based mechanisms are energy-efficient, making them suitable for resource-constrained WSNs. On the other hand, trust-encryption hybrids are designed to scale across large, heterogeneous IoT networks. However, dense network environments can reduce detection accuracy, as RSSI and Time Difference of Arrival (TDOA) techniques may misclassify legitimate nodes due to signal interference or overlapping transmission paths. Trust models are also vulnerable to manipulation, where malicious nodes inflate their trust scores or evade detection. Many countermeasures struggle with dynamic or mobile IoT devices, instead relying on static configurations that have problems under changing conditions. Cryptographic methods, especially the ones using symmetric key protocols, face scalability challenges and high overhead, with the risk, that compromising a single node could affect the entire network. Artificial intelligence-based solutions, while promising, often suffer from computational intensity and optimization difficulties, such as with Particle Swarm Optimization (PSO) methods, which can converge prematurely on local optima, reducing detection accuracy. Additionally, approaches like resource testing and watchdog monitoring, although effective, can drain battery-powered sensors during verification.

2.5 Related Work

Sybil attacks remain one of the more disruptive types of threat in decentralized and distributed systems, allowing a single attacker to control several false identities and therefore corrupt decision-making, resource distribution and trust mechanisms of the network. As previously stated, in the context of the Internet of Things, the Sybil attacks might take on a variety of characteristics. This shows the variety of Sybil behaviours and emphasizes the challenge of developing countermeasures that work successfully under IoT constraints of limited computation power, energy constraints, varied node capabilities and inconsistent connectivity. These challenges motivate future research of different detection systems and prevention mechanisms that can function under such constraints.

2.5.1 Local, Collaborative and Mobility Detection

One main aspect of Sybil defence is focused on collaborative detection within a local neighbourhood. Rajadurai and Gandhi (2020) propose a fuzzy-logic-based neighbour verification mechanism in which nodes use overlapping observations from neighbouring monitors to identify fraudulent peers. This method decreases false positives and overhearing overhead in Mobile Ad hoc NETwork (MANET) environments by making detection decisions close to the source of observations.

Nodes in mobile IoT networks, due to the mobility, can show inconsistencies in signal strength, making position prediction and interval estimation more difficult. For mobile IoT networks, a distributed detection scheme using received signal strength indications (RSSI) by Yan et al. (2023) computes expected signal intervals in a first round and flags deviations in a second. It is lightweight and because of the distribution across the edge nodes, choosing whatever nodes have better performance and no other tasks, the method is scalable, as it does not rely too heavily on centralized servers. To decrease memory overhead, past data is not stored and while RSSI can fluctuate, affecting detection reliability, the paper uses a theoretical RSSI range, based on RSSI observations. An earlier approach by Jamshidi et al. (2017) uses mobility analysis, in which mobility-based watchdogs track node movements over short periods of time, assign labels and discover Sybil nodes by clustering identities with nearly identical movement histories, indicating a single operator behind multiple nodes. These systems outperform static detection baselines in terms of true- and false-positive rates in mobile sensor networks, but their effectiveness decreases when Sybil nodes leave their groups due to collisions, resulting in observation gaps. To prevent this, some systems include processes that forget old labels, preventing outdated trajectory information from causing false positives (Fig. 2.3).

Vehicular ad hoc network (VANET) research explores the use of Proof-of-Location methods paired with blockchain-based immutability to limit Sybil exploitation. A recent approach by Khatri, Lee & Nam (2024) requires vehicles to solve puzzles generated by Road Side Units (RSU) before submitting pseudonymous, hash-verified locations. This approach restricts the submission of multiple false identities and locations by limiting one puzzle per vehicle, while reducing infrastructure strain when compared to trajectory-reconstruction baselines, as it uses smart contracts on existing frameworks such as Ethereum. The location information is immutably stored using smart contracts, managed by the RSUs, which maintain a blockchain for storing the location information of neighbouring vehicles, ensuring the data is tamper-resistant and verifiable, while protecting the privacy of the vehicles.

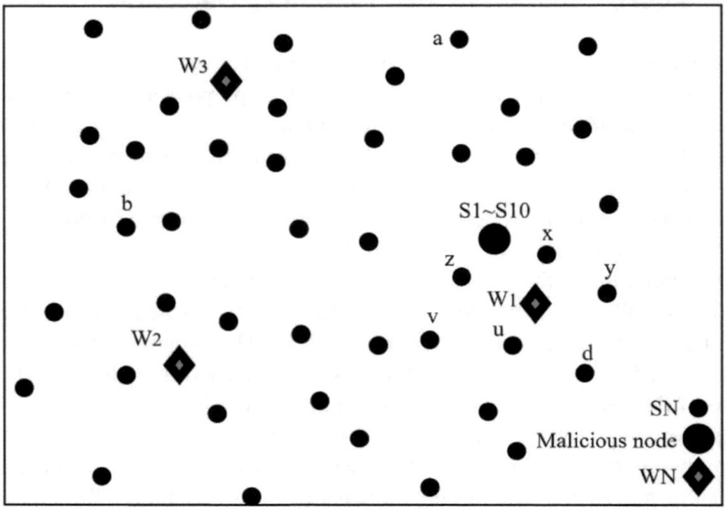

Fig. 2.3 An example of deploying nodes in the first execution round of the algorithm from Jamshidi et al. (2017). (© 2016 Elsevier. Reprinted with permission)

2.5.2 Trust Modelling

In low-power IoT networks, a Sybil-Free Metric-based routing protocol trustworthiness scheme (SF-MRTS) proposed by Hussain et al. (2024) distributes trust management by having nodes evaluate neighbouring nodes using trust tables based on energy, honesty, selfishness and expected transmission count (ETX), which describes the expected total number of packet transmissions required for the successful transmission of a packet along that path (Yang & Wang, 2008).

Game-theoretic penalties and rewards affect node behaviour, forcing nodes to cooperate, resulting in high reported detection rates and packet delivery during attacks. The initial trust computation needs a significant amount of resources, but the strategy consumes less energy over time while maintaining a high packet delivery ratio (Hussain et al., 2024).

According to the survey on Sybil countermeasures in IoT by Arshad et al. (2021), energy-efficient RSSI and trust hybrids are especially suited for restricted IoT nodes, as they provide scalability across varied deployment scenarios while maintaining low energy costs. However, these systems have shortcomings, including RSSI volatility due to environmental factors, susceptibility to trust manipulation and collisions, with another difficulty being computational and optimization challenges.

2.5.3 Identity Anchoring and Trust Ledger Design

In addition to detection, other research aims to entirely prevent Sybil nodes from being created, by raising the economic penalty of identity creation. The Rechained scheme, proposed by Bochem & Leiding (2021), extending on the earlier presented Unchained protocol, uses this strategy by tying identity registration to on-chain deposits, enabling offline verification and integration with self-sovereign identity systems. It makes creating multiple false identities exceedingly costly for attackers, due to an adjustable price of identity creation, while reducing the computational impact on low-power IoT devices by offloading the main computations to public blockchains. While Proof-of-Burn, in which the price is sent to a wallet with no known private key, is presented as the most secure method for this approach, due to the limited supply of certain cryptocurrencies, funds are suggested to be sent to network operators or charities instead, rather than destroying them.

The TrustChain is a different approach by Otte, de Vos & Pouwelse (2020) that incorporates Sybil resistance directly into the ledger design, replacing global consensus with locally validated and parallel transactions. Each agent maintains their own personal chain of bilateral transactions, generating their own genesis blocks and keeping account of each transaction they were involved in, with each block holding only one transaction rather than multiple. After each transaction, both parties sign and add another block to their own chain, with each block pointing back to the counterpart's last block to prevent block reorganization and removal. This also leads to the identification of replay attacks, in which agents reuse counterpart signatures to reproduce beneficial transactions. These attacks are discovered when agents examine the correctness of other agents' transaction chains and notice several blocks with identical outgoing pointers. The TrustChain becomes Sybil resistant by using a NetFlow algorithm that limits the impact of false identities through the usage of a trust system in which users who contribute to the community acquire trust while freeriders are penalized. Freeriders are identified by the weight of how much work they have done compared to the effort spent by others, allowing service rejection to uncooperative agents who worked less than a certain limit and limiting their long-term influence (Fig. 2.4).

An approach by Kelamat, Queralta & Westerlund (2023) uses partition tolerance, with robotic systems, that function reliably even when parts of the network are disconnected. It uses IOTA smart contracts, in which the embedded Byzantine fault tolerance is used to be more resilient towards false nodes. The architecture based on directed acyclic graphs (DAG) strengthens the connectivity as this architecture is more flexible and scalable with a low resource impact due to the low computational overhead. A more recent approach using smart contracts is SybilP-SIoT (Dayyani & Abbaspour, 2024), which combines smart contract based owner control with a Bayesian inference model, which judges the target node in paths between verification and desired nodes, decentralizing trust. These trust paths, due to having multiple, lead to noise resistance and scalability. To prevent Sybil node creation, there is a game theoretic part which controls access owners using a cost and benefit function (Fig. 2.5).

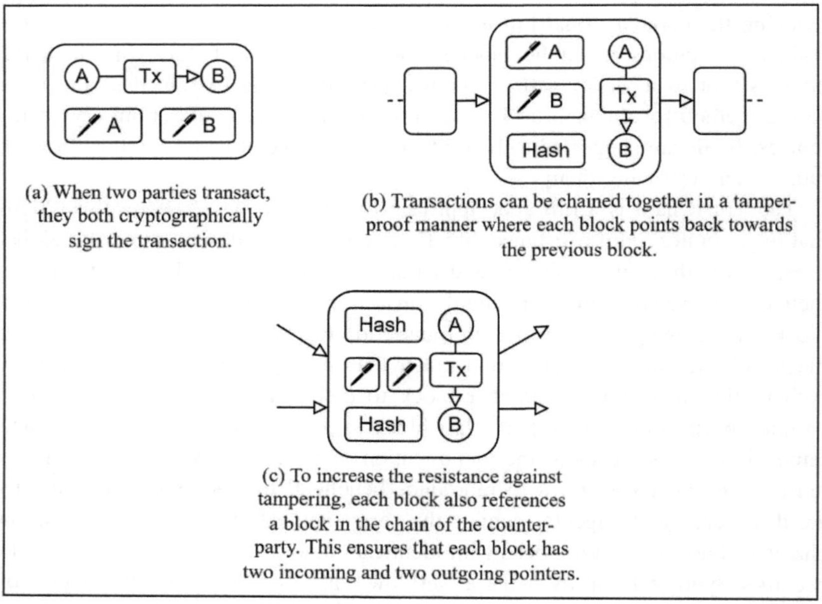

(a) When two parties transact, they both cryptographically sign the transaction.

(b) Transactions can be chained together in a tamper-proof manner where each block points back towards the previous block.

(c) To increase the resistance against tampering, each block also references a block in the chain of the counter-party. This ensures that each block has two incoming and two outgoing pointers.

Fig. 2.4 Example of the block creation process when agents A and B have participated in a transaction, adapted from Otte, de Vos & Pouwelse (2020). (© 2017 Elsevier. Reprinted with permission)

2.5.4 Consensus-Level Robustness

Sybil attacks at the consensus layer pose a serious threat to decentralized systems. Afzaal, Imram & Janjua (2023) propose a blockchain-based Trust and Transactions Chain (TTC) consensus protocol to reduce fraud in crowdsourcing systems. Their approach prevents double spending and Sybil attacks by selecting leaders and validators through a trust model based on deposit ratio, block generation rate, validation rate, and waiting rate.

More recently, a protocol by Xu, Shahraki & Chilamkurti (2024) aims to secure Byzantine Fault Tolerant (BFT) consensus in permissionless blockchain. The protocol uses a bootstrapping method with random endorsement groups and Boneh-Lynn-Shacham (BLS) signatures to maintain low verification costs. Due to the requirement of identity endorsement and deposits, the system fights Sybil attacks while maintaining decentralization. This protocol also consumes less computing power and is suitable for IoT devices, as it avoids energy intensive methods like Proof-of-Work. Additionally, the communication complexity does not grow exponentially and because there is no third party necessary for authentication, nodes can join the network if they are meeting the requirements, allowing for decentralized participation, despite less powerful devices.

In regards to multi-agent systems, a lightweight consensus mechanism proposed by Dong et al. (2022) uses random label values assigned to the agents to validate neighbour agents, providing energy-efficient operation at scale. Outliers get reduced influence due to the Sybil detection using internal relationships. The model separates Sybil parent and child nodes, which are the false identities created by Sybil nodes, using message patterns instead of the physical fingerprints, as the latter consumes more computational power and energy (Fig. 2.2).

2.5.5 Trustless and Distributed Detection Signals

Some defences avoid centralized control, instead relying on network-layer measures as indicators. Stokkink et al. (2023) propose SybilSys, which uses network latency patterns to avoid Sybil attacks and assumes nodes with comparable latencies are Sybils. It is a trustless Sybil detection method that relies only on network latency and does not require trust between nodes. Another mechanism TrafficJamTrigger detects message flow interference to identify flow patterns that suggest Sybil behaviour. It creates round-trip time (RTT) measurement message flows and uses binary classifiers to detect RTT increases. With this strategy,

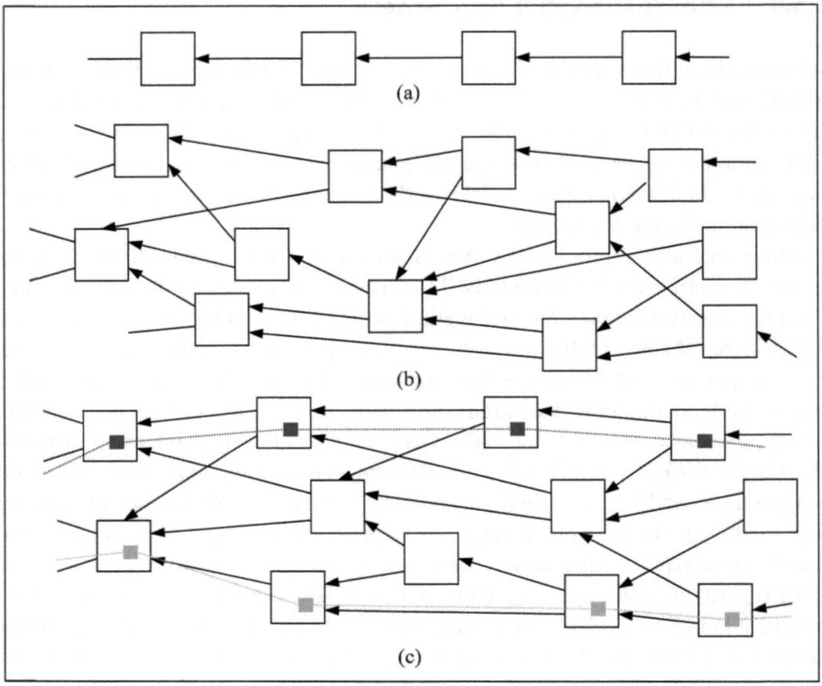

Fig. 2.5 Illustration of (a) traditional blockchain, (b) IOTA Tangle, and (c) two-layer ISCP architecture where two possible chains anchored to different Table nodes are highlighted. (Adapted from Keramat, Queralta & Westerlund (2023). Licensed under CC BY 4.0)

attackers can only increase latency rather than decrease it, making manipulation difficult and allowing the system to function even when the majority of the network is made up of Sybils.

A different and more recent approach by Liu et al. (2025) uses subgraph-based feature propagation, which captures local transaction patterns around each address. The approach creates two-layer transaction subgraphs around each address to record the local network topology and behaviour patterns. From these subgraphs, 75 features are extracted, which are used for feature propagation and fusion in the subgraph layers to show coordinated Sybil attack behaviour including star-shaped transaction patterns, where one main node sends assets to the other nodes and crowded activity timelines.

2.5.6 Power Scaling and Active Sybil Attacks

As mentioned above, power scaling attacks manipulate transmission power and use mobility to bypass detection metrics. ScatterID, an approach proposed by Huang et al. (2019) detects power-scaling Sybil attacks in which attackers modify the transmission strength of the false Sybil nodes to make them appear to have different signal profiles. Using backscatter tags to generate multipath reflections that change dependent on a node's position and movement, the approach normalizes these signal profiles to reduce power-based differences, allowing the system to detect Sybil identities, despite their different signal profiles.

A recent study by Netto, Cholez and Ignat (2025) addresses active Sybil attacks that combine the false identity creation with active disruptions which avoid detection. While in these attacks the semantically correct responses undermine distributed hash table lookups, the proposed Sybil-Resistant DHT-Store (SRDHT-Store) overcomes this by using XOR distance, computing where the nodes should be located, which reduces the influence of the malicious nodes.

2.5.7 Simulation Frameworks

For evaluation and experimentation, the LUNES simulation (Serena, D'Angelo & Ferretti, 2021) offers a parallel and distributed simulation environment for blockchain networks. Each layer of the simulation is modelled separately to have a more fine tuned simulation for each. This layered approach is used later in the methodology, due to the ability to evaluate the results more in detail, as the agents used in the modelling help with flexibility and extensibility due to different behaviour and their modular structure. Additionally, a probabilistic generating function analysis (PGFA) model by Hafid, Hafid & Samih (2021), estimates failure probabilities under varying Sybil counts, committee sizes and resiliency thresholds, offering a tractable means to set safety margins. A table provides an overview of the related work mentioned (Table 2.1).

Table 2.1 Overview of related work

Paper	Solution
Jamshidi et al. 2017	Watchdog nodes
Huang et al. 2019	Multi-path Signal Signatures
Rajadurai, Ghandi 2019	Collaborative verification system with fuzzy logic
Otte, de Vos, Pouwelse 2020	Trustchain with NetFlow, addresses freeriding
Bochem, Leiding 2021	Blockchain Identity Cost Barrier
Serena, D'Angelo, Ferretti 2021	Agent-based simulator of blockchains
Dong et al. 2022	Attack-resistant consensus algorithm
Yan et al. 2023	Mobility-based RSSI Sybil Detection and collaborative edge computing
Stokkink et al. 2023	DecentralizedLatency-BasedDetectionand TrafficJamTrigger
Keramat, Queralta, Westerlund 2023	Partition tolerant, Byzantine tolerant, IOTA and ROS2
Khatri, Lee, Nam 2024	Proof-of-Location & Smart Contracts
Dayyani, Abbaspour 2024	SybilPSIot based on signed networks and web of trust
Xu, Shahraki, Chilamkurti 2024	Endorsement-based bootstrapping protocol
Hussain et al. 2024	Trust-based system on secure paths, mechanisms based on game theory
Liu et al. 2025	Subgraph-based feature propagation and fusion approach
Netto, Cholez, Ignat 2025	Region-based queries

Research Design 3

This study follows the Design Science Research (DSR) paradigm, which seeks to address relevant, real-world problems through the creation and evaluation of innovative artifacts (Hevner et al., 2004; Peffers et al., 2007). DSR is particularly well-suited to contexts such as Sybil-resistance in M2M payment networks, where both the problem space and the solution space are complex, multi-faceted, and dynamic. As emphasised by Peffers et al. (2007), DSR aims to produce both a viable artifact and knowledge about its design, applicability and performance. In this work, the artifact takes the form of a layered multi-agent system (MAS) and blockchain-based architecture that integrates multiple detection cues, economic deterrence mechanisms and resilience-enhancing strategies. In positioning this research within the broader DSR tradition, the study also considers recent advances in handling complexity in DSR, as outlined by Tuunanen et al. (2024), who propose design echelons as a way to manage interdependencies across multiple design layers. This perspective is particularly relevant given that the proposed architecture spans edge-level detection, trust management and payment-layer protocols, all of which interact in non-trivial ways.

Furthermore, the evaluation of the artifact is informed by the Framework for Evaluation in Design Science (Venable et al., 2016), which stresses the importance of aligning evaluation activities with the research goals, artifact maturity and available resources. Given that the proposed system is evaluated in a simulated environment that is constrained by computational resources and the feasibility of modelling large-scale IoT deployments, the evaluation strategy follows an ex-ante simulation-based approach, focusing on measurable detection performance, payment reliability, cost overhead, resilience and ledger integrity (Fig. 3.1).

K. A. Stiller, *Securing Peer-to-Peer Identities in IoT Systems Using Blockchain and Multi-Agent Systems with an Outlook on M2M Payment Applications*, BestMasters, https://doi.org/10.1007/978-3-658-51520-1_3

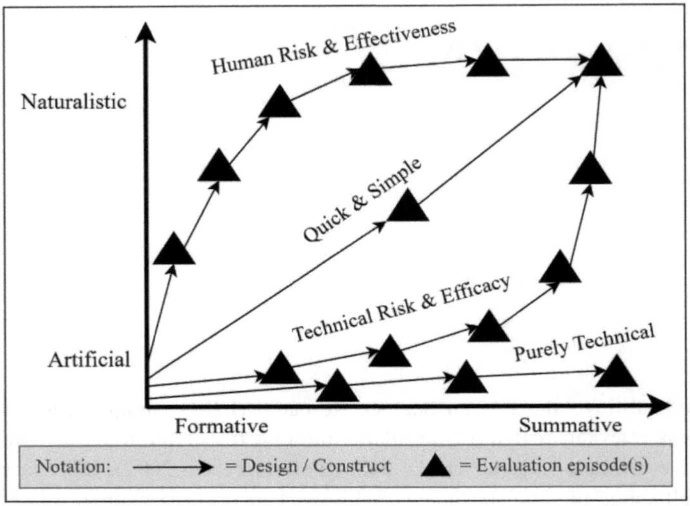

Fig. 3.1 Framework for Evaluation in Design Science with evaluation strategies from Venable et al., (2016). Licensed under CC BY 4.0.

3.1 Design Science Stages

Activity 1 Problem Identification and Motivation

Problem identification and motivation Sybil attacks in M2M payments present a multi-vector challenge that cannot be reliably countered by a single detection approach under IoT constraints. The problem is heightened by the need to both detect and economically deter attackers while keeping micro-transactions viable.

Activity 2 Objectives for Solution

Define the objectives for a solution The proposed system should

(a) improve Sybil detection across multiple variables
(b) maintain payment success under attack
(c) deter identity inflation economically
(d) remain feasible for resource-constrained IoT devices

Activity 3 Design and Development

Design and development A layered MAS and blockchain architecture is developed, combining lightweight RSSI with mobility checks, deposit-based identity control and local trust logs.

Activity 4 Demonstration

Demonstration The system as a proof-of-concept is evaluated in a modular, agent-based Python simulation, incorporating both detection approaches by themselves to compare to the proposed approach and different simulation parameters to isolate the impact of different scenarios.

Activity 5 Evaluation

Evaluation Using the FEDS-informed simulation evaluation, the system's performance is assessed across detection accuracy for both True Positive and False Positive Rates, payment performance, cost/overhead, resilience and ledger integrity metrics.

Activity 6 Communication

Communication The findings are positioned for both academic audiences and practitioner audiences via this thesis.

Methodology 4

4.1 Objectives

In a machine-to-machine (M2M) payment environment, human oversight is minimal. Therefore the decision-making must be automatic and robust against manipulation. Sybil attacks pose a particularly persistent threat, exploiting social infiltration, mobility patterns and active misbehaviour. Under the constraints of Internet of Things (IoT) devices, it is difficult for single detection mechanisms to reliably detect and prevent them. Papers like the SybilPSIoT by Dayyani & Abbaspour (2024) who use a hybrid approach as well as the paper by Stokkink et al. (2023), who not only layer two approaches but suggest their final proposed approach to be combined with other Sybil attack defences, inspire a combination of different approaches in this paper. That is why the objective of this thesis is to design a layered architecture combining distributed multi-agent system (MAS) anomaly detection with a selective, lightweight blockchain identity layer.

While MAS-based intrusion detection systems (IDS) can improve coverage and avoid single points of failure, they have to be lightweight enough for resource-limited nodes and blockchain-based identity schemes like Rechained and TrustChain, add verifiable cost to identity creation and can operate in a permissionless environment. But each introduces their own trade-offs like user costs, revocation delays or replay and reset risks. By combining the strengths of both, it becomes possible to avoid large-scale Sybil creation economically while preserving the viability of frequent micro-transactions. In addition, the architecture must keep computational and storage overhead low enough to support high-rate micro-transactions, balancing cost and deterrence so that attacks become economically unattractive without making legitimate operation uneconomical.

K. A. Stiller, *Securing Peer-to-Peer Identities in IoT Systems Using Blockchain and Multi-Agent Systems with an Outlook on M2M Payment Applications*, BestMasters, https://doi.org/10.1007/978-3-658-51520-1_4

4.2 Threat Model and Attack Scenarios

The threat model anticipates attackers capable of generating and coordinating large numbers of Sybil identities, which may be static or mobile and exhibit traits designed to evade specific detection layers. These Sybils may remain passive, blending into the network until activated or behave actively by issuing repetitive, low-value transactions to distort payment flows and mimic plausible activity. Some variants manipulate attributes such as movement speed, identity appearance or signal strength to game selection metrics and evade detection.

In open, permissionless environments, attackers can cheaply spawn new identities at a pace that outstrips centralized revocation. Without economic friction, detection alone risks being overwhelmed. To counter this, the system introduces blockchain-based deposits and reciprocity-driven trust scoring to raise the cost of Sybil creation and reward cooperative behaviour. These mechanisms are adapted to the IoT context to remain lightweight and avoid exploitable resets. Detection layers based on Received Signal Strength Indicator (RSSI) consistency, mobility patterns and fusion of multiple signals each target specific Sybil traits, but are individually insufficient. Given the heterogeneous, intermittently connected, and resource-constrained nature of the environment, the attack surface remains broad. The overarching goal is to limit the breadth of Sybil infiltration by making large-scale identity creation costly and detectable and to reduce the depth of Sybil influence by preventing unverified or uncooperative nodes from dominating routing, trust, or payment decisions. These goals shape the methodology with an early-stage, device-local anomaly detection to constrain attacker influence quickly, a lightweight blockchain registration to impose costs and reciprocity-based trust scoring to reward cooperation. Lastly the simulation-driven evaluation measures the detection of attackers and the resilience of the payments network against the combinations of Sybil.

4.3 Model Structure

This work adopts a layered multi-agent system combined with selective blockchain integration to address the diverse vectors of Sybil attacks in IoT-enabled payment environments. The approach begins with fully local, lightweight anomaly detection, uses blockchain-backed identity and trust only when necessary and finally incorporates economic deterrence mechanisms and behavioural accountability. The architecture is designed to remain working within the computational, storage and energy constraints typical for IoT devices.

At the foundation of the system is an edge-level anomaly detection base inspired by the work of Yan et al. (2023). Each edge node runs simple, independent detectors that operate without central coordination, ensuring that detection costs scale at worst linearly with the number of devices. The first and primary signal is a RSSI interval analysis, in which nodes exchange probe messages and compare expected versus observed received signal strength intervals. This method has been shown in IoT contexts to offer scalable detection, though its accuracy can degrade under high mobility or environmental noise. Complementing the RSSI analysis is a watchdog node check, looking for Sybil sets, inspired by the approach proposed by Jamshidi et al. (2017). The two approaches should complement each other as RSSI is known to be fast, low overhead, effective in static or low mobility environments but sensitive to noise, multipath fading and environmental interference. Meanwhile mobility based approaches like the watchdog approach is robust against signal noise, effective in dynamic environments where movement patterns reveal Sybil behaviour but requires longer observation time and is less effective in static scenarios. This fusion approach uses the complementary strengths of RSSI and mobility analysis, mitigating the weaknesses of each other under different conditions.

The final core component addresses payment-aware routing and economic deterrence. Trust scores are updated in an event-driven manner to reduce computational load. Periodic settlements are recorded both in the smart contract and in the local trust ledger, ensuring accountability. Game-theoretic incentive structures link uncooperative behaviour to higher costs, reducing the utility of Sybil nodes even if they evade detection. When local detectors indicate elevated suspicion, the system selectively uses its blockchain-based trust and identity layer. To avoid reliance on costly global consensus, nodes maintain local, append-only trust ledgers in the style of TrustChain (Otte, de Vos Pouwelse, 2020). These record bilateral interactions and compute reciprocity-based trust balances without resorting to computationally expensive max-flow calculations. Newly registered identities are subject to temporary trust penalties to discourage repeated reputation resets. The benefits are robustness by using complementary detectors, stability through temporal smoothing and cost efficiency by limiting expensive blockchain operations to cases where physical evidence already indicates likely Sybil nodes. Here, new identities are registered through a minimal smart contract requiring an adjustable security deposit, inspired by the Rechained framework by Bochem and Leiding (2021). Systems like Ethereum's Proof-of-Stake and reputation-based ledgers use this principle as well, using deposits or collateral to align incentives and discourage malicious behaviour.

This transition marks a shift from unconditional participation to conditional trust enforcement, where flagged nodes must register with a deposit, face revocation delays and earn back trust through cooperative behaviour. The TrustChain acts like a gatekeeper, selectively applying friction to deter Sybil strategies without compromising the accessibility of the broader system for honest participants. It goes from qualitative trust dynamics to quantitative cost modelling, where deposits, transaction fees and revocation penalties are tracked to simulate real-world incentives. By embedding economic friction into the participation model, Layer 5 evaluates whether the deterrence strategies of Layer 4 translate into sustainable, scalable defence in practice. This mechanism serves multiple purposes being economic deterrence as Sybil identities become costly to maintain and auditability because the ledger provides a historical record of identity behaviour. This layer also aligns with the Design Science principle of rigour as it builds on economic theory, cryptographic primitives and distributed systems research to create a mechanism that is both theoretically sound and practically implementable.

The simulation is implemented within a modular, agent-based simulator. Inspired by the LUNES framework but designed from scratch for this purpose, the simulator models explicit peer-to-peer networking, node mobility, payment flows and lightweight blockchain operations. Its modularity allows individual components to be removed or modified to quantify their impact. The simulation is scaled to several nodes, having flexible parameters across deposit sizes, trust update rates, mobility models and diverse Sybil strategies, ensuring that results capture the trade-offs inherent in balancing detection accuracy, system overhead and cost.

4.3.1 Algorithmic Components

The proposed Sybil attack mitigation framework for machine-to-machine payment networks combines multiple algorithmic components designed to detect, resist and penalize malicious identity creation, while preserving payment efficiency and ledger integrity. At its foundation lies an RSSI interval detection process. In the initial stage, edge nodes calculate an expected signal strength interval for each peer and in a subsequent stage, compare observed values against these expectations, flagging peers whose values persistently deviate. To improve robustness in mobile scenarios, the mechanism is extended with machine learning-based position prediction, enabling more stable interval estimates despite environmental variability. This is complemented by a mobility consistency check that tracks short-horizon trajectories and clusters nodes exhibiting near-identical movement histories, a pattern indicative of co-controlled identities.

Additional detection signals are derived from a latency-based trustless probing mechanism inspired by Web3 principles. Here, periodic micro-probes are injected into the network and binary classifiers detect flow interference patterns, converting the results into suspect scores through a thresholding process that does not require global coordination. Identity control and accountability are enforced through a minimal smart contract design based on the Rechained model, enabling identity registration, deposit staking and revocation. Offline verifiable proofs are simulated by issuing signed receipts and revocation lag is explicitly modelled to capture realistic operational delays. Local trust records follow the TrustChain architecture, in which each agent maintains an append-only, cryptographically signed ledger of bilateral interactions. Reciprocity-driven ranking, inspired by network flow models, is used to down-rank freeriders, while replay and fork detection is implemented via pointer duplication and cross-link validation. Routing and payment scheduling follow an SF MRTS-inspired model, where trust is computed as a function of factors including energy expenditure, honesty, selfishness and expected transmission count. Game-theoretic reward and penalty mechanisms dynamically adjust node transmission rates and payment eligibility. High-trust peers are prioritized by the scheduler, while low-trust or unproven nodes may be denied participation. An optional proof-of-location subsystem, following VANET principles, introduces RSU-like beacons into the simulation.

Each identity is issued a single location puzzle per period, with pseudonymous attestations committed to a contract, allowing analysis of verification accuracy under varying RSU densities. Finally, active Sybil mitigation techniques inspired by SR DHT Store are applied at the routing layer, incorporating region-based or XOR-distance-biased lookups, multiple disjoint query paths and early termination strategies reinforced by the suspect scoring mechanism.

4.4 Metrics

To evaluate the effectiveness of this combined system, several metrics are used. The detection performance is measured through true positive (TPR) and false positive rates (FPR), time to detection and the area under the receiver operating characteristic curve (AUC). Cost and overhead measurements are collected for both attackers and the system. For attackers, relevant costs include identity deposits and the resources lost through failed attack attempts.

4.5 Scope and Limitations

The evaluation focuses on progressively enhancing the proposed defence architecture in a series of configurations, beginning with minimal detection and culminating in the complete multi-layer stack. This staged approach enables a clear attribution of performance changes to individual components while also illustrating their cumulative effect. The Baseline configuration operates without any Sybil defence, providing a lower bound for attack impact and serving as the reference point for all other scenarios. The Edge-Only configuration introduces lightweight RSSI-based anomaly detection at the device level, capturing coarse inconsistencies in link quality. Building on this, the RSSI and mobility combination aims to overcome weaknesses and detect Sybils with each strengths. Beyond detection, the Identity and Local Trust configuration integrates a minimal deposit-based blockchain identity layer with append-only local trust logs, deterring mass identity creation and promoting reciprocity in payments without the cost of global consensus.

The scope is limited to an agent-based simulation framework capable of modelling heterogeneous, resource-constrained IoT nodes with intermittent connectivity. While the simulation environment aims to capture realistic network dynamics, certain factors remain abstracted. While the incremental configurations allow for an in depth analysis of all situations, the study does not exhaustively explore parameter tuning for all detection thresholds, deposit amounts or trust update policies as these are fixed to representative values to maintain comparability. As a result, the findings speak primarily to the relative trends between configurations rather than the exact absolute performance in deployment, acting more as a proof-of-concept rather than a real world example. In addition, the study is bounded by practical computational and timely constraints. All simulations were implemented in Python and executed on a single laptop system, which limits the feasible scale of experiments. While the framework supports hundreds of heterogeneous agents interacting under different network and mobility conditions, scaling to millions of nodes, comparable to global IoT deployments is beyond available resources. Instead, the focus is on moderate-scale scenarios sufficient to observe behaviour, evaluate detection accuracy and compare defence configurations. This choice ensures tractable run times and interpretability of results, but it also means that findings may not directly capture performance bottlenecks or adversarial strategies that only emerge at extreme scale.

Implementation 5

This chapter describes how the artifact outlined in Chap. 4 was instantiated. The implementation is a modular, agent-based simulator written in Python that models edge detection, mobility grouping, identity registration, trust propagation and payments. This chapter shows the design rationale, core algorithms and simulator structure.

5.1 Simulated Environment

The environment is realized as a set of Agent classes and specialized nodes placed on a 2D grid. The simulation is a discrete simulation executed in rounds. In each round the Agent can freely move around the grid, limited only by predetermined parameters for their velocity. Sybil nodes might try spoofing the new position, strengthen their antennas to influence the RSSI calculations or changing their identity. After the movement of the nodes is finished, the respective layer implementation computes the metrics for the round.

The Agents are a representation of dynamic or mobile nodes moving around the network. The Sybil nodes are a special case of Agent class that redefines movement and RSSI calculation by potential spoofing. The Sybil agents may also introduce identity changes to the nodes *address* parameter.

K. A. Stiller, *Securing Peer-to-Peer Identities in IoT Systems Using Blockchain and Multi-Agent Systems with an Outlook on M2M Payment Applications*, BestMasters, https://doi.org/10.1007/978-3-658-51520-1_5

```
class Agent:
    def __init__(self, address, position):
        self.address = address self.base_address = address
        self.position = np.array(position, dtype=float)
        self.last_position = self.position.copy()

    def move(self, velocity):
        self.last_position = self.position.copy() self.position
        += np.array(velocity, dtype=float)

    def get_rssi(self, edge_pos, tx_power=1.0, alpha=2):
        d = np.linalg.norm(self.position - np.array(edge_pos))
        return calculate_rssi(tx_power, d, alpha)
```

Listing 5.1 Agent class

The special nodes on the network are Edge and Watchdog nodes. The edge nodes are a different type of agent, static and are responsible to calculate the η ratio of RSSI with the monitored agent and the second edge node. The Edge nodes see the whole network and can communicate with all other nodes. Each round two random Edge nodes are selected for Sybil agent detection using Layer 1.

```
class EdgeNode:
    def __init__(self, position): self.position =
        np.array(position, dtype=float)

    def compute_rssi_ratio(self, agent, other_edge): rssi_self =
        agent.get_rssi(self.position) rssi_other =
        agent.get_rssi(other_edge.position) return rssi_other /
        rssi_self if rssi_self != 0 else np.inf
```

Listing 5.2 Edge node class

The other type is Watchdog node. The Watchdog node are statically placed on the grid to cover the area of the network. The Watchdog nodes monitor Agents in their range that was defined at the beginning of the simulation. The watchdogs can communicate with other watchdogs that are within their range. Their purpose is to detect node that move in clusters.

```
class WatchdogNode:
    def    __init__(self,    position,    bit_label,    range=10.0):
        self.position    =    np.array(position,    dtype=float)
        self.bit_label = bit_label self.range = range
        self.moving_history = {}
    def detect_neighbors(self, agents):
        return [ a for a in
            agents
            if np.linalg.norm(a.position - self.position) <= self
                .range
        ]
```

Listing 5.3 Watchdog node class

5.2 Simulation Architecture

As mentioned above, the simulation consists of 5 layers. The first layer uses a computationally light RSSI physical layer approach, doing a simple first test in detecting Sybil nodes. The second layer is using watchdog nodes (WN) that detect identical movements in groups and identity changes. These two layers are being combined to create a weighted synergy, in a third layer. The fourth detection and prevention layer uses TrustChain-like ideas and economic deposits inspired by the Rechained approach to identity creation, but in order to keep it economically affordable, this is used only for suspicious nodes. The final layer introduces micropayments to add economic costs per transaction and ensure that even when Sybils get through, they cannot harm the system or spam and manipulate transactions (Table 5.1).

Table 5.1 Simulation Architecture

Layer	Focus	Task
Layer 1	RSSI-based	Captures physical signal anomalies to flag suspicious identities
Layer 2	Mobility-based	Identifies coordinated movement patterns typical of Sybil nodes
Layer 3	Fusion logic	Combines RSSI and mobility scores with adaptive weighting and smoothing
Layer 4	Trust	Introduces deposits and penalties to economically deter Sybil behavior
Layer 5	Economic Results	Evaluates real-world cost and transactional resilience of the system

5.2.1 Layer 1

The first layer of the Sybil defence framework operates at the edge of the network, using RSSI-based signal characteristics to identify suspicious identities. The idea is that Sybil identities often originate from the same physical device and therefore tend to exhibit consistent RSSI ratios when observed from multiple edge nodes. The framework conducts two rounds of RSSI sampling and compares the ratios to a theoretically derived safe interval. A stable ratio suggests consistent positioning, while large deviations indicate tampering or abnormal mobility and deviations from this interval may indicate Sybil behaviour or abnormal mobility. Intelligent algorithms are used to predict node positions and refine the expected RSSI range, improving detection accuracy.

While the approach by Yan et al. (2023) uses a two-round RSSI sampling process and the LSTM model for mobility prediction, this simulation introduces modifications to enable broader experimentation. The goal is to evaluate Sybil detection logic across multiple approaches, including RSSI-based methods, without constraining the simulation to a fixed temporal pattern. This design choice allows for more flexible integration of alternative techniques and reflects the dynamic nature of M2M payment networks, where continuous or asynchronous communication is common. That is why this simulation replaces the two-round structure with a continuous detection logic, allowing for more flexible and iterative analysis of RSSI behaviour. Additionally, the computationally more intensive LSTM model is changed with a computationally less heavy approach. To replace the original paper's LSTM mobility prediction, this simulation uses a lightweight linear extrapolation strategy implemented in a PositionPredictor class. These adaptations are not intended to replicate the original framework but rather to extend its principles into the modular simulation. By doing so it aims to evaluate the strengths and limitations of RSSI-based Sybil detection under realistic constraints and operational conditions relevant to decentralized M2M payment systems.

RSSI Calculation

Based on the paper by Yan et al. (2023), the RSSI between node i and edge node j is modelled, following the Jakes model, linking distance and signal strength.

$$R_i^j = \frac{k * P_x}{\left(d_i^j\right)\alpha}$$

k is a constant, while P_x is the transmit power, d_i^j is the distance between nodes and α is the path-loss exponent. In open field scenario the *alpha* would be equal to 2, in other scenario it could change, e.g. for dense urban scenarios *alpha* is usually set to 2,7. The distance is calculated using the Euclidean distance equation.

$$d_i^j = \sqrt{(x_j - x_i)^2 + (y_j - y_i)^2}$$

The calculate_rssi() function uses the equation with a 1e-6 guard to prevent a zero-division blow-up if a denominator hits zero due to floating-point imprecision (Table 5.2).

```
def calculate_rssi(tx_power, distance, alpha=2): return
    tx_power / ((distance + 1e-6) ** alpha)
```

Listing 5.4 RSSI computation

Edge Node Model

After determining the RSSI for each agent and edge pair, these values are used to compare the relative distances between observation locations. This serves as the foundation for detecting Sybil node activity, in the Edge Node model. If one edge node registers a much weaker signal than another at that moment, the model uses the ratio of these measurements as a clue to the node's likely location. The EdgeNode class models a fixed observation point and can compute the RSSI ratio η between itself and another edge node for a given agent, using the measurements R_1^{ir} and R_2^{ir} from two distinct edges for the same agent.

$$\eta_x = \frac{R_1^{ir}}{R_2^{ir}} = \left(\frac{d_1^i}{d_2^i}\right)^{\alpha}$$

A large deviation of η_x outside the expected interval $I = [Imin,Imax]$ derived from geometry and mobility constraints for η_x, flags the node as suspicious. These bounds represent the maximum and minimum expected RSSI ratios given the agent's velocity and position relative to the edge nodes.

$$i = \left[\frac{-2A - B + \sqrt{B^2 - 4AC}}{2A - B + \sqrt{B^2 - 4AC}}, \quad \frac{2A - B + \sqrt{B^2 - 4AC}}{-2A - B + \sqrt{B^2 - 4AC}}\right]$$

$$A = 4x_1^2c^2 - 4r^2c^2$$

$$B = -4x_1c\left(x_1^2 + y_1^2 + c^2 - r^2\right)$$

$$C = \left(x_1^2 + y_1^2 + c^2 - r^2\right)^2 + 4r^2c^2$$

A, B and C, which encode geometric constraints based on the agent's position relative to the edge nodes and its maximum velocity, are computed in the calculate_ABC() function, producing the coefficients from agent and edge positions along with the assumed velocity bound to use the calculated values in calculate_eta_interval() which gives the bounds against which η_x is compared (Table 5.2).

```
def compute_rssi_ratio(self, agent, other_edge): rssi_self =
    agent.get_rssi(self.position) rssi_other =
    agent.get_rssi(other_edge.position) return rssi_other /
    rssi_self if rssi_self != 0 else np.inf
```

Listing 5.5 RSSI Ratio η_x computation in EdgeNode class

```
def calculate_ABC(agent_pos, edge1_pos, edge2_pos, vmax):
    c1, c2 = edge1_pos, edge2_pos c =
    np.linalg.norm(c1 - c2) / 2.0
    midpoint = (c1 + c2) / 2.0 x_rel,
    y_rel = agent_pos - midpoint r = vmax

    if c == 0:
        c = 1e-6
    A = (4 * x_rel**2 - 4 * r**2) / (c**2)
    B = -4 * x_rel * c * (x_rel**2 + y_rel**2 + c**2 - r**2)
    C = (x_rel**2 + y_rel**2 + c**2 - r**2)**2 + 4 * (r**2) * (c
        **2)
    return A, B, C
```

Listing 5.6 Computation of coefficients A, B and C

```
def calculate_eta_interval(A, B, C): sqrt_term =
    np.sqrt(max(B**2 - 4*A*C, 0)) denom1 = 2*A - B +
    sqrt_term denom2 = -2*A - B + sqrt_term lower = (-
    2*A - B + sqrt_term) / (denom1 or 1e-6) upper = (2*A
    - B + sqrt_term) / (denom2 or 1e-6) return
    min(lower, upper), max(lower, upper)
```

Listing 5.7 Computation of interval I for η_x

Identifier Change Tracking

In addition to RSSI calculations, the paper by Yan et al. (2023) includes identifier change tracking. Since some Sybil nodes quickly change their IDs, the Identity-Tracker class maintains an address history for each physical device and indicates changes between rounds. The system runs two detection rounds, collecting each node's shared identity in the first and then again in the second. If a node displays a different ID the second time, but its key matches the same device, it is marked as suspicious. A genuine new device would exhibit distinct RSSI patterns, while a Sybil node would create a RSSI signature identical to the previous one. Unlike the paper by Yan et al. (2023) this thesis uses more than two rounds and because in this simulation no new members join, there is no base station test and devices with identical IDs are directly flagged as Sybil nodes. The code begins by creating an empty history to store the key and the list of IDs that each device has used. The record() function determines a stable key for devices, so that regardless of ID changes, the key can be used to look up the device's history to compare the addresses.

```
def record(self, agent, round_num):
    key = agent.base_address if hasattr(agent, "base_address") else
        agent.address
    if key not in self.history:
        self.history[key] = []
    self.history[key].append(agent.address)
```

Listing 5.8 Records the agent's current ID for this round

```
def compare(self, agent, round_num):
    key = agent.base_address if hasattr(agent, "base_address") else
        agent.address
    if key not in self.history: return
        "Unknown"
    identities = self.history[key] if
    len(set(identities)) == 1:
        return "Same"
    else: return
        "Changed"
```

Listing 5.9 Compares the agent's ID to see if it has changed

Detection Logic

The detect_sybil() function brings together RSSI bounds, mobility limits and identity change checks. These computations are combined in the detection logic to form the combined decision in the RSSI layer.

```
def detect_sybil(agent, edge1, edge2, round_num, tracker,
    predictor=None, vmin=0.1, vmax=1.0):
    tracker.record(agent, round_num) identity_status =
    tracker.compare(agent, round_num) eta_new =
    edge1.compute_rssi_ratio(agent, edge2)

    A1, B1, C1 = calculate_ABC(agent.last_position, edge1.
        position, edge2.position, vmax=vmax)
    I_min_vmax, I_max_vmax = calculate_eta_interval(A1, B1, C1) A2,
    B2, C2 = calculate_ABC(agent.last_position, edge1.
        position, edge2.position, vmax=vmin)
    I_min_vmin, I_max_vmin = calculate_eta_interval(A2, B2, C2)

    I_lower = I_min_vmin / 2
    I_upper = I_max_vmax * 2

    if identity_status == "Changed": return
        ("Sybil", 2)

    if I_lower <= eta_new <= I_upper:
        return ("Normal", 1)
    else: return ("Sybil",2)
```

Listing 5.10 Sybil detection decision logic (RSSI)

Table 5.2 Notations used in the equations

Symbol	Description
u_i	A normal member node or a malicious node
e_j	The *j*-th edge node
r	Measurement round index
Rij,r	RSSI value from u_i to e_j in the *r*-th round
k	Environment/antenna constant
P_x	Transmit power of u_i
dj_i	Distance between u_i at (x_i,y_i) and e_j at (x_j,y_j)
α	Path-loss exponent
ηx	RSSI Ratio
$I = [I\text{min}, I\text{max}]$	Admissible interval for η
A,B,C	Coefficients for admissible η interval

Note: The paper by Yan et al. (2023) reuses the symbol x for unrelated purposes being the spatial coordinates in the Euclidean Distance (x, y), a round index in η_x and in P_x as the transmit-power variable. For accuracy, the equations here are reproduced exactly as in the source.

5.2.2 Layer 2

Complementing the RSSI-based detection layer, this simulation implements a mobility-based Sybil detection stage directly adapted from Jamshidi et al. (2017). In the original algorithm, watchdog nodes (WN) monitor the movement of nearby identities over multiple rounds, appending a fixed bit-label to each observed node's history in that round. When a node moves between WNs, its accumulated history is transferred so that the sequence is preserved. After P monitoring rounds, each WN groups identities with identical bit-label sequences and any group whose size meets or exceeds the threshold Ts is flagged as a Sybil set, as Sybil nodes tend to exhibit identical movement patterns because they are controlled by the same entity.

Watchdog node placement

The success rate of this strategy is highly dependant on the positioning of the watchdog nodes. For effective detection of the Sybil nodes, the watchdogs should cover the whole area of the network. The watchdogs should not be isolated, because the strategy depends on watchdogs sharing information between each other. The uncovered areas are practically a blind-spot in which the Sybil nodes can act however they want to without any threat of detection. On the other side, overfilling the area with watchdog nodes might result in higher false positive rate. For the purpose of the simulation it splits the grid into equal squares. Each square is covered by a single watchdog. On the edges of the square watchdogs can communicate with the watchdogs in the neighbouring squares, providing some communication without any overlap in the covered areas. This placement provides some blind-spots that could be abused by Sybil nodes. Covering the whole area could be quite expensive, therefore this placement might get close to reality, where the whole network area could not be covered either. This placement covers approximately 80% of the total network area.

```
wn_range = field_size / 8.0 watchdogs = []
for i in range(int(field_size / wn_range)):
    for j in range(int(field_size / wn_range)):
        watchdogs.append(WatchdogNode([(i + 0.5) * wn_range,
        (j + 0.5) * wn_range], bit_labels[i ],
        range=wn_range))
```

Listing 5.11 Watchdog placement

Mobility

Following the approach by Jamshidi et al. (2017), each WN detects neighbours within its range and updates their bit-label histories. These histories are exchanged between WNs when nodes move between coverage areas. Before monitoring begins, WNs are positioned in the simulation space and a spacing routine ensures that no two WNs are closer than a minimum distance, preventing excessive overlap in coverage areas and ensuring more even monitoring as the paper assumes that the WNs are well-distributed. Then each WN is assigned a fixed bit-label that it will append to the history of any node it observes in a round, a position in the simulation space, a detection range and an initially empty moving_history dictionary for mapping node IDs to their accumulated bit-label strings. Each round, a WN identifies which agents are within its range using the detect_neighbors() function which is used in every monitoring round to decide which nodes receive the WN's bit-label for that round.

At each round each WN detects its current neighbours using detect_neighbors () and for any new neighbour IDs not already in its moving_history, the WN checks other WNs to see if they have been tracking that ID. If so, it retrieves and removes the existing history from the other WN using the history transfer step from the original algorithm. All current neighbours have the WN bit-label appended to their history string for this round. This process builds up a sequence of bit-labels for each node

```
    def detect_neighbors(self, agents):
        return [ a for a in agents if np.linalg.norm(a.position -
            self.position) <= self.
                range
        ]
```

Listing 5.12 Neighbour Detection

over the rounds, even if the node moves between WNs. This preserves continuity across WNs and is the key to detecting Sybil sets in a mobile environment.

```
def update_moving_history(watchdogs, agents):
    request_lists = {} for i, wn in
    enumerate(watchdogs):
        neigh     = wn.detect_neighbors(agents) new_ids =
        [a.address for a in neigh if a.address not in
        wn.moving_history]
        request_lists[i] = new_ids

    responses = { i: {} for i in range(len(watchdogs)) }
    for i, new_ids in request_lists.items(): for nid in
    new_ids: for j, other in enumerate(watchdogs):
                if j == i:
                    continue
                if nid in other.moving_history:
                    responses[i][nid] = other.moving_history.pop(
                    nid) break

    for i, wn in enumerate(watchdogs): for
        nid in request_lists[i]:
            wn.moving_history[nid] = responses[i].get(nid, "")
        for a in wn.detect_neighbors(agents):
            wn.moving_history.setdefault(a.address, "")
            wn.moving_history[a.address] += wn.bit_label
```

Listing 5.13 Movement History

After several rounds, each WN groups nodes by their complete bit-label string and flags large groups. Here, Ts is the group-size threshold and any group of identical histories with size equal or larger is considered a Sybil set. This output is used as the binary score of the mobility layer in the combined detection framework, to determine if a node is a Sybil node or not.

```
def detect_sybil_sets(watchdogs, Ts):
    sybil_sets = [] for wn in watchdogs: label_groups = {}
    for node_id, label in wn.moving_history.items():
            label_groups.setdefault(label, []).append(node_id)
        for group in label_groups.values(): if
            len(group) >= Ts:
                sybil_sets.append(group)
    return sybil_sets
```

Listing 5.14 Threshold

5.2.3 Layer 3

While the individual RSSI-based and mobility-based detectors each capture specific aspects of Sybil node behaviour, their strengths vary depending on environmental conditions. This thesis implements a fusion that weights the detection scores, smooths their outputs across rounds and selectively moves suspicious cases to the higher-layer trust mechanism. The RSSI-based and mobility-based detectors are first combined using a weighted decision based on confidence scores.

Combined Decision

This thesis presents a simplified proof of concept for the confidence-based fusion. While the general idea of adaptive weighting is implemented, the current approach does not dynamically derive confidence from environmental parameters. Instead, it assumes higher trust in mobility-based detection due to the mobile nature of the environment in this simulation. The fusion score is then computed using the weighted input.

$$Sfused = Wrssisrssi + Wmob\,Smob$$

The weights calculation is then used in the code, with the ability to extend it. While the current implementation uses static confidence values per input, the structure allows for future enhancements where confidence scores can be dynamically updated over time, based on historical trends, environmental factors or additional metrics.

To avoid one-off anomalies caused by noise or transient misclassifications, the fusion keeps a short sliding window of recent fused scores per node. The final decision is based on the moving average where W is the size of the smoothing window.

```
Def _adaptive_weights(self, confidences):
    total_conf = sum(confidences.values()) or 1.0 return {k:
    (confidences[k] / total_conf) for k in confidences
        }
```

Listing 5.15 Weights calculation

```
Def _temporal_smooth(self, node_id, score):
    dq = self.score_history.setdefault(node_id, deque(maxlen=self
        .smoothing_window))
    dq.append(score) return
    np.mean(dq)
```

Listing 5.16 Smoothing

```
def fuse(self, node_id, s_rssi, s_mob, c_rssi=1.0, c_mob=1.0):
    confidences = {"c_rssi": c_rssi, "c_mob": c_mob} weights =
    self._adaptive_weights(confidences) fused_score =
    (weights["c_rssi"] * s_rssi + weights["c_mob"] * s_mob)
    smooth_score = self._temporal_smooth(node_id, fused_score) if
    smooth_score >= self.Tf: decision = "Sybil" escalate =
    (smooth_score >= (self.Tf + 0.2))
    else:
        decision = "Normal" escalate
        = False
    return decision, smooth_score, escalate
```

Listing 5.17 Combined decision calculation

5.2.4 Layer 4

The trust layer combines the economic deterrence from the Rechained approach by Bochem and Leiding (2021) with the behavioural accountability inspired by the TrustChain (Otte, de Vos & Pouwelse, 2020), forming a dual-trust enforcement mechanism that penalizes identity resets while reinforcing honest interactions. This layer introduces the blockchain-inspired trust enforcement system that simulates the structured ledger which Layer 5 later builds on, to evaluate the economic implications of participation under adversarial conditions. This layer serves as a proof-of-concept for a blockchain-based Sybil defence mechanism, including trust enforcement and identity persistence modelled using the simulated identity ledger. While the full blockchain implementation including distributed consensus, cryptographic identity and peer validation was not developed due to time constraints, the current simulation captures the basic logic and economic deterrence principles that would support such a system.

This approach has two purposes, as it discourages Sybil attackers by making the creation of identities costly and unprofitable, as well as providing a structured recovery path for false positives that are genuine nodes that were misclassified due to momentary deviations. Within this layer, flagged identities are documented in a local trust ledger, with deposits acting as both a barrier and a behavioural signal. This phased approach avoids penalizing honest nodes prematurely, instead moving only those who indicate continuous suspicion. By requiring deposits for participation, the system assures that identity generation is no longer free and that the cost of carrying out Sybil attacks grows linearly with the quantity of false identities, making these types of attacks economically irrational. In high-noise environments, especially those involving machine-to-machine payments, the cost of false negatives rises rapidly. As automated machines lack human control, it is important to be more cautious when detecting Sybil identities. This requires a more intensive detection method, even if it leads to more false positives. Under real-world conditions it is possible to expect even higher noise levels, reinforcing the importance of robust and flexible detection systems.

Identity Ledger

When a node's suspicion score $s_{fused}(t)$ exceeds the threshold T_{fusion}, it is flagged as a potential Sybil. If the suspicion score stays persistent through out multiple rounds or reaches a higher threshold $T_{fusion} + \delta$, the node is added to the trust layer, triggering the TrustChain mechanism, where the node must register a deposit to continue, following the Rechained-inspired deterrence model. The deposit is the core mechanism to deter potential Sybil attackers due to the heightened costs. The register_identity() function ensures that a node can only register if it has not been recently revoked. Revoked nodes are nodes, which access to the system was taken away, because of their past uncooperative behaviour. It records the registration event, stores the deposit, and applies a temporary trust penalty.

The trust layer serves not only as a deterrent for Sybil attackers but also as a behavioural proving ground for misclassified nodes. Cooperative behaviour gradually earns trust and rewards, while malicious or evasive actions drain the stake. If a node misbehaves or resets its identity, this function logs the revocation and enforces a delay before another registration is allowed, as the revocation delay defines the minimum number of rounds a node must wait after being revoked before it can register again, serving as a deterrent against rapid identity cycling.

```
def register_identity(self, node_id, round_num, deposit=None):
    deposit_amt = deposit if deposit is not None else self.
        base_deposit
    if node_id in self.revocations and round_num < self.
        revocations[node_id]:
         return False
    self.chains.setdefault(node_id, []).append(("REGISTER",
        round_num, deposit_amt))
    self.deposits[node_id] = deposit_amt self.trust_penalty[node_id] =
    round_num + self.penalty_window return True
```

Listing 5.18 Identity registration

```
def revoke_identity(self, node_id, round_num):
    self.chains.setdefault(node_id, []).append(("REVOKE", round_num,
        self.deposits.get(node_id, 0)))
    self.revocations[node_id] = round_num + self.revocation_delay
    return True
```

Listing 5.19 Identity revoking

This creates a real economic cost for repeated identity resets, making Sybil attacks financially unattractive. Once a node is added to the trust layer, its identification is handled using a blockchain-based ledger. Each identity must register with a deposit, and any revocation results in a cool down period before another registration is allowed. To prevent immediate trust following identity resets, the penalty window, meaning the duration during which the trust score is reduced, restricts immediate restoration of full access. As this temporarily lowers the trust of the node, all attempts to participate during this time are penalized, ensuring that trust is restored only once the revocation delay has expired. When the penalty period ends, the node regains full trust status.

5.2.5 Layer 5

While the payment layer operates as a permissionless and open ledger, allowing all nodes to transact freely by default, this freedom is conditional on behavioural integrity. Once a node exhibits suspicious activity as determined by its fused suspicion score, it no longer has unrestricted access. Layer 4 establishes a behavioural firewall that constrains Sybil actors and incentivizes cooperative behaviour. However, trust alone does not capture the full cost of participation or disruption. To measure the practical viability of the system under adversarial pressure, Layer 5 introduces an economic lens that quantifies the financial burden imposed on both attackers and honest nodes.

Economic Evaluation

Layer 5 serves as the final evaluation layer of the Sybil defence framework, focusing on the financial impact and operational performance of the system under Sybil and honest agents. While previous layers focus on detection, grouping and trust enforcement, this layer measures the cost of participation and disruption, providing a practical view on the effectiveness of the entire Sybil detection and prevention approach. This layer simulates transactional behaviour between agents, tracking both successful and failed transactions and measuring the cumulative cost caused by honest participants and Sybil attackers. By assigning a transaction fee and enforcing deposit requirements for flagged identities, the system introduces real economic friction that discourages Sybil's uncooperative behaviour while maintaining accessibility for legitimate nodes. The system is initialized with configurable transaction fees and deposit requirements. It maintains account balances for each node and tracks performance metrics throughout the simulation.

```
def __init__(self, trustchain, tx_fee=0.01, deposit_min=1.0):
    self.trustchain = trustchain
    self.tx_fee = tx_fee
    self.deposit_min = deposit_min
    self.balances = {} self.metrics
    = {
        'fees_collected': 0.0,
        'tx_success': 0,
        'failed_tx': 0,
        'attacker_cost': 0.0,
        'honest_cost': 0.0,
    }
    self.active_sybils = set()
return True
```

Listing 5.20 Initialization

Each transaction checks whether the sender has enough balance to pay the fee. If the sender is flagged as a Sybil, the system enforces deposit registration before allowing further participation. This mechanism ensures that Sybil identities incur a growing cost with each transaction, while honest nodes pay only the base fee.

When initiating a transaction, the system first ensures that both sender and receiver have valid accounts, with all agents, including Sybil adversaries, required to meet a minimum deposit threshold. This deposit acts as a financial gatekeeper, preventing unregistered Sybil identities from participating without incurring an upfront cost. Once registered, Sybil agents are tracked to avoid repeated deposit charges, but they continue to accumulate costs through transaction fees.

The transaction process itself is designed to simulate realistic economic behaviour. If the sender lacks sufficient balance to cover the transaction fee, the attempt is rejected and logged as a failed transaction. This mechanism prevents zero-cost spamming and reinforces the need for financial accountability. This behaviour can be penalized to prevent the spamming, resulting in lower trust and higher costs for nodes participating in it. Successful transactions deduct the fee from the sender's balance, credit the receiver, and update performance metrics accordingly.

```
def process_transaction(self, sender, receiver, amount, round_num ,
   is_attacker=False): self.ensure_account(sender, self.deposit_min
   if is_attacker else 0.0)
    self.ensure_account(receiver, 0.0)

    if is_attacker and sender not in self.active_sybils:
         self.trustchain.register_identity(sender, round_num,
             deposit=self.deposit_min)
         self.active_sybils.add(sender) self.metrics['attacker_cost']
         += self.deposit_min

    if self.balances[sender] < self.tx_fee:
         self.metrics['failed_tx'] += 1 return
         False

    self.balances[sender] -= self.tx_fee
    self.metrics['fees_collected'] += self.tx_fee if
    is_attacker:
         self.metrics['attacker_cost'] += self.tx_fee
    else: self.metrics['honest_cost'] += self.tx_fee

    self.balances[receiver]  +=  amount
    self.metrics['tx_success']   +=   1
    return True
```

Listing 5.21 Transaction process

The system distinguishes between attacker and honest roles when recording costs. Both attackers and false positive attackers pay both the deposit and the transaction fees. The deposit and transaction fees are tracked for both attacker and honest agents to have an understanding of how economically feasible both the micropayments and the Sybil defence would be. For the most effective systems the ratio of honest nodes costs to Sybil nodes costs should approach zero.

5.3 Metrics Collection

The last puzzle piece for the implementation is the collection of the metrics. Different layers require different metrics to be collected for the evaluation. The metrics collector collect the true positives and false negatives for each Sybil node type with total Sybil nodes detected. It also tracks the specific ID of nodes that were suspected by the algorithm to be Sybil adversaries. The tracked score is the confidence of the algorithm for the suspected node to be Sybil. Each layer has its own distinct MetricsCollector, so the results from different layers do not influence each other. The MetricsCollector is also responsible to compute the metrics for the evaluation such as True Positive Rate, False Positive Rate, Area Under Curve tracking the ratio of TPR and FPR. During the result summary the class can also compute the ratio of number Sybils of specific type caught to the total type of Sybil nodes of said type.

```
class MetricsCollector:
    def __init__(self, name=""):
        self.name = name self.tp = self.fp =
        self.tn = self.fn = 0 self.scores = []
        self.labels = [] self.computation_times =
        [] self.sybil_detection_times = {}
        self.by_sybil_type = {
            "speed": {"TP":0, "FN":0, "total":0},
            "identity": {"TP":0, "FN":0, "total":0},
            "rssi": {"TP":0, "FN":0, "total":0},
        }
```

Listing 5.22 Metrics collect initialization

The private helper function *register sybil type* takes in the prediction result of a round and the Sybil node that was detected. The provided agent is expected to be an instance of a Sybil node. Based on the type of the Sybil node instance the function than record the total number of the Sybil node type detected. Based on, whether the detection was correct or not, it either records a True Positive or False Negative for each type of Sybil Node. If it is a first round in which this particular Sybil Node was detected, the function also record the number of the round.

```
def _register_sybil_type(self, agent, predicted, round_num):
    if not isinstance(agent, SybilAgent):
        return
    if agent.speed_boost:
        self.by_sybil_type["speed"]["total"] += 1 if predicted:
        self.by_sybil_type["speed"]["TP"] += 1 else:
        self.by_sybil_type["speed"]["FN"] += 1
    if agent.identity_changer:
        self.by_sybil_type["identity"]["total"] += 1 if
        predicted: self.by_sybil_type["identity"]["TP"] +=
          1
        else: self.by_sybil_type["identity"]["FN"] += 1
    if agent.rssi_spoofer:
        self.by_sybil_type["rssi"]["total"] += 1 if predicted:
        self.by_sybil_type["rssi"]["TP"] += 1 else:
        self.by_sybil_type["rssi"]["FN"] += 1
    if predicted and agent.address not in self.
       sybil_detection_times:
        self.sybil_detection_times[agent.address] = round_num
```

Listing 5.23 Sybil classification

The *record* takes a result of detection as a set of parameters and computes the statistic for the round. The input parameters are:

1. score → confidence of the algorithm that the node is Sybil
2. label → whether the node actually is Sybil or not
3. predicted → whether the algorithm predicted the node to be a Sybil
4. agent → the node under detection
5. round num → the number of round in which this detection run

The function counts false and true positive and negatives and calls the *register sybil type* to more accurately record the type of Sybil node that was correctly flagged.

```
def record(self, score, label, predicted, agent, round_num):
    self.scores.append(float(score))
    self.labels.append(int(label)) if
    label == 1:
        if predicted: self.tp += 1 else: self.fn += 1
        self._register_sybil_type(agent, predicted, round_num
            )
    else:
        if predicted: self.fp += 1 else:
        self.tn += 1
```

Listing 5.24 Result recording

The *compute metrics* function computes the TPR, FPT and AUC rates. The TPR is defined as a number of True Positives over the total amount of Sybil nodes entering the recorder, True Positives and False Negatives. The FPR is defined as a number of True Positives over the total amount of non-Sybil nodes entering the recorder, True Negatives and False Positives. Additionally, it produces *avg time* for each round of detection and number of round on average in which the Sybil nodes got flagged.

```
def compute_metrics(self):
    tpr = self.tp / (self.tp + self.fn) if (self.tp + self.fn
        ) > 0 else 0.0 fpr = self.fp / (self.fp + self.tn) if
    (self.fp + self.tn
        ) > 0 else 0.0
    auc = roc_auc_score(self.labels, self.scores) if len(set(
        self.labels)) > 1 else 0.0
    avg_time = np.mean(self.computation_times) if self.
        computation_times else 0.0
    avg_detection_round = np.mean(list(self.
        sybil_detection_times.values())) if self.
        sybil_detection_times else 0.0
    return tpr, fpr, auc, avg_time, avg_detection_round
```

Listing 5.25 Metrics computation

The last function is *print summary*, which gets the computed metrics from the instance of the MetricsCollector and formats the results. It focuses on TPR, FPR and AUC, including also catch rates for all types of Sybil nodes. This formatting for output was chosen, because it is easy to read, yet it provides all relevant information for the experiment. Some stored metrics like *avg detection round* is not displayed because it is not relevant to this experiment, but it could be proven useful for future works.

```
def print_summary(self):
    tpr, fpr, auc, avg_time, avg_det = self.compute_metrics()
    print(f"=== {self.name or 'METRICS'} ===")
    print(f"TPR={tpr:.3f}, FPR={fpr:.3f}, AUC={auc:.3f},
       AvgTime(ms)={avg_time*1000:.3f}") for k
    in   ["speed","rssi","identity"]:   tot   =
    self.by_sybil_type[k]["total"]     tp     =
    self.by_sybil_type[k]["TP"]
        rate = (tp/tot*100) if tot>0 else 0.0 print(f" {k}:
        caught {tp}/{tot} ({rate:.2f}%)")
    print()
```

Listing 5.26 Results formating

The implementation provides a simple, but effective framework for setting up the simulation for the experiment. The modular features of the implementation enable easy stacking of the detection mechanisms implemented as layers. The agent classes can be generated at will of the person running the experiment, providing easy scaling of the experiment. The MetricsCollectors gather the results that are ready to display after the simulation has been run and the experiment can be easily evaluated.

Results and Analysis

6

This section presents an analysis of the detection performance across the four layers, each incorporating distinct mechanisms to identify Sybil agents. Metrics such as True Positive Rate (TPR), False Positive Rate (FPR) and Area Under the Curve (AUC) are used to evaluate effectiveness across multiple simulation runs. This chapter evaluates the implemented artifact against the objectives defined in the research design and the metrics mentioned in the methodology. The evaluation follows the FEDS framework (Venable et al., 2016) with an ex-ante, simulation-based strategy. The experiments will be evaluating the effectiveness of the approach given different parameters, while comparing them to the single RSSI and Mobility detection.

6.1 Experimental Setup

Table 6.1 Experimental Parameters

Parameters	Values
Network size	100 × 100m2
Number of normal nodes	N = 100, 200, 300, 400, 500
Number of Sybil nodes	S = 10, 20, 30, 40
Number of edge nodes	E = 8, 12
Number of monitoring rounds	R = 20, 60, 100

K. A. Stiller, *Securing Peer-to-Peer Identities in IoT Systems Using Blockchain and Multi-Agent Systems with an Outlook on M2M Payment Applications*, BestMasters, https://doi.org/10.1007/978-3-658-51520-1_6

To evaluate the system's performance across a range of adversarial and cooperative conditions, the simulator introduced in the previous chapter is used. This setup allows for systematically tests on the layered defence architecture under controlled parameters and configurations (Table 6.1). The simulation environment consists of 100 nodes, of which 10 are designated as Sybil attackers with different characteristics, some of which can show multiple of. In addition to the core network, 8 edge nodes are included to simulate gateway behaviour and external interactions. Each experiment runs for 20 simulation rounds, with a fixed random seed equal to 4 for pseudorandom generator to support reproducibility. Economic parameters are set to reflect realistic constraints and incentives. Each honest node begins with a default deposit of 10 units, which governs its ability to participate in transactions and trust mechanisms, while Sybil nodes begin with 50 units in order to have more room to engage in the network. To explore the impact of each defence mechanism, the simulation is differentiated into five different versions (Table 6.2).

Table 6.2 Simulation Architecture

Version	Task
Baseline	No defences are active, the system operates without any protective layers
Layer 1	Only the RSSI detection with the edge nodes and the identity check
Layer 2	Only the mobility detection using the watchdogs
Layer 3	Fusion of the RSSI and the mobility detection using the weighted decision making
Full Simulation	Added layer 4 and layer 5 ledgers to examine the costs and successful transactions

Throughout each simulation run, the system logs a set of outputs which include per-round records of detections, payment transactions, trust updates and committee decisions. This enables the analysis of system dynamics, attacker impact and defence efficacy across configurations. By structuring the experiments in this way, each layer's contribution can be isolated and evaluated both independently and in combination. The resulting data forms the basis for the performance metrics and comparative analysis presented in the following chapters.

6.2 Detection Performance

The baseline configuration, which lacks any defence mechanisms, shows no meaningful detection. Without active monitoring or trust mechanisms, Sybil nodes operate freely and the system remains blind to Sybil behaviour (Table 6.3).

Table 6.3 Performance under base parameters

Version	TPR	FPR	AUC
Baseline	0.000	0.000	0.500
Layer 1	0.835	0.615	0.610
Layer 2	0.665	0.379	0.643
Layer 3	0.800	0.530	0.712

6.2.1 Layer 1

The first layer relies only on the RSSI ratios in order to compare it to the combined detection. This detection method achieves a TPR of approximately 0.84, indicating that only some Sybils are correctly identified but the reliance on noisy local data results in a FPR of around 0.62 as well, reflecting occasional misclassification of honest nodes. Across runs, the overall AUC reaches 0.61.

Listing 6.1 N = 100

```
=== Layer-1: RSSI ===
TPR=0.835, FPR=0.615, AUC=0.610
speed: caught 33/40 (82.50%) rssi:
caught 116/140 (82.86%) identity:
caught 118/120 (98.33%)
```

Compared to a configuration with 500 nodes, the detection improves. But detection does not grow with node amount as a run with N = 300 results in a TPR of around 0.79 but also a decreased FPR of approximately 0.49. The AUC however, is actually higher an AUC of approximately 0.65. While increasing node count seems to enhance detection capabilities due to richer data and more observable interactions, the improvement is not strictly proportional. As shown at N = 300, detection metrics sometimes drop compared to N = 100 or N = 500, suggesting that intermediate densities may introduce noise or reduce the clarity of behavioural patterns.

Listing 6.2 N = 500 shows stronger detection

```
=== Layer-1: RSSI ===
TPR=0.855, FPR=0.600, AUC=0.628
speed: caught 31/40 (77.50%) rssi:
caught 129/140 (92.14%) identity:
caught 137/140 (97.86%)
```

Listing 6.3 N = 300 shows weaker detection

```
=== Layer-1: RSSI ===
TPR=0.785, FPR=0.486, AUC=0.649
speed: caught 91/100 (91.00%) rssi:
caught 97/140 (69.29%) identity:
caught 120/120 (100.00%)
```

6.2.2 Layer 2

The second layer uses only the mobility-based detection for comparison purposes as well. This layer has a TPR of approximately 0.67 and a FPR of approximately 0.38. This detection method is more conservative, detecting less Sybils but also flagging less honest nodes as Sybil agents. The AUC is slightly above the AUC seen in the first layer, indicating better differentiation between honest and Sybil agents, despite the overall lower TPR. From the result it is visible that this layer concern itself significantly less about the changing speed of Sybil nodes. The changing speed is not an indicator of common move pattern this layer monitors.

Listing 6.4 N = 100

```
=== Layer-2: Mobility ===
TPR=0.665, FPR=0.379, AUC=0.643
speed: caught 15/40 (37.50%) rssi:
caught 95/140 (67.86%) identity:
caught 99/120 (82.50%)
```

Like the first layer, this method also improves with the higher nodes configuration of N = 500 which is not indicative of a positive relationship as the same round of N = 300 results in weaker detection.

Listing 6.5 N = 500 shows stronger detection

```
=== Layer-2: Mobility ===
TPR=0.730, FPR=0.669, AUC=0.530
speed: caught 24/40 (60.00%) rssi:
caught 94/140 (67.14%) identity:
caught 110/140 (78.57%)
```

Listing 6.6 N = 300
shows weaker detection

```
=== Layer-2: Mobility ===
TPR=0.475, FPR=0.577, AUC=0.449
speed: caught 36/100 (36.00%) rssi:
caught 46/140 (32.86%) identity:
caught 72/120 (60.00%)
```

6.2.3 Layer 3

The third layer introduces the combined decision making of the first and second layer, using the weighted score. While this layer has a lower TPR than the first layer, the FPR is visibly reduced, which is also indicated in the AUC, which is higher than both of the methods by themselves.

Listing 6.7 N = 100

```
=== Layer-3: Fusion === TPR=0.800,
FPR=0.530, AUC=0.712 speed: caught
31/40 (77.50%) rssi: caught 115/140
(82.14%) identity: caught 118/120
(98.33%)
```

Similar to layer 1 and 2, this approach shows a more stronger detection at 500 nodes, because its own detection logic is based on the first two layer. During the 300 nodes run the layer is overall doing worse than the first layer and is being influenced by the second layer FPR, due to the slight favouritism in the weighted decision-making leaning towards the second layer.

Listing 6.8 N = 500
shows stronger detection

```
=== Layer-3: Fusion === TPR=0.865,
FPR=0.688, AUC=0.687 speed: caught
25/40 (62.50%) rssi: caught 123/140
(87.86%) identity: caught 137/140
(97.86%)
```

Listing 6.9 N = 300
shows weaker detection

```
=== Layer-3: Fusion === TPR=0.705,
FPR=0.524, AUC=0.599 speed: caught
87/100 (87.00%) rssi: caught 81/140
(57.86%) identity: caught 120/120
(100.00%)
```

6.2.4 Comparison between Layers

Across all configurations, the three-layered detection framework shows strengths and limitations at each stage. Layer 1, relying only on RSSI ratios, consistently achieves high true positive rates, especially at larger node counts, but suffers from higher false positive rates due to the inherent noise in signal strength data. Layer 2, based on mobility patterns, offers a more conservative approach. The lower TPR is offset by a reduced FPR, suggesting it is better at avoiding misclassification of honest nodes, though it struggles to detect more evasive Sybil agents. Layer 3, which fuses the outputs of the first two layers through weighted decision-making, strikes a balance between sensitivity and specificity. While its TPR occasionally falls below that of Layer 1, it benefits from a consistently higher area under the curve, indicating improved and more accurate overall detection. However, its performance is sensitive to the biases of the underlying layers, especially when mobility-based detection contributes disproportionately to the final decision.

This layered comparison highlights the value of fused detection, while also underscoring the importance of calibrating inter-layer influence to avoid amplifying weaknesses. Across all layers, identity-based Sybil nodes were consistently detected with high accuracy, often exceeding 0.97, which shows the reliability of static identity verification mechanisms. RSSI-based Sybils showed variable detection rates, with the first layer performing best due to its direct reliance on signal strength analysis. Mobility-based Sybils were the most difficult to detect, especially in Layer 2, where detection rates dropped significantly at lower node counts. This suggests that mobility patterns alone may not be sufficient for robust Sybil identification, especially when legitimate nodes show similar movement behaviour. For a better visualization, the Receiver Operating Characteristic (ROC) curve plots the TPR and FPR against each other (Fig. 6.1).

Besides more nodes, the detection accuracy also shifts when there are more Sybil attackers present. In a network with many attackers, especially the RSSI-based approach shows a high TPR of 0.830 (Fig. 6.2), but this comes at the cost of a relatively high FPR of 0.592 and a modest AUC of 0.619. The declining AUC suggests that while the system is effective at catching attackers, its overall discriminative power weakens as the attacker population grows which could be due to increased signal interference and overlapping RSSI profiles among legitimate and malicious nodes.

The breakdown of the performance of Layer 1 shows that it is very strong in identifying identity-based Sybils, catching 492 out of 500 and performs well in both speed-based and RSSI-based detection categories but the higher FPR means

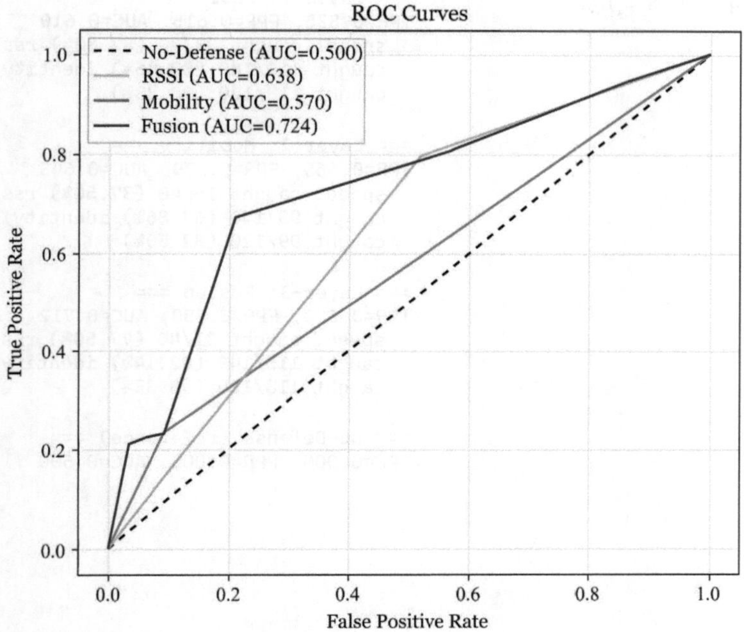

Fig. 6.1 Comparison of ROC curves

that many honest nodes are misclassified. Layer 2 on the other hand, once more offers a more conservative detection strategy. Its TPR drops to 0.646, but the FPR also decreases to 0.414, resulting in an AUC of 0.616 which is slightly below Layer 1 but with improved precision. This layer has mostly trouble with the speed-based Sybils, catching only 124 out of 260 but its lower FPR makes it an important component in reducing collateral damage to honest nodes, which is why Layer 3 achieves a balanced TPR of 0.794 and an FPR of 0.511, with the highest AUC of 0.714. This indicates that while it may not match Layer 1 in raw detection rate, it offers a better overall classification performance. The fusion layer benefits from the complementary strengths of RSSI and mobility analysis, catching 0.85 of speed-based Sybils and over 0.85 of RSSI-based ones, while having the same high accuracy for identity-based detection as Layer 1 (Fig. 6.3).

Listing 6.10 N = 100

```
=== Layer-1: RSSI ===
TPR=0.835, FPR=0.615, AUC=0.610
  speed: caught 33/40 (82.50%) rssi:
  caught 116/140 (82.86%) identity:
  caught 118/120 (98.33%)

=== Layer-2: Mobility ===
TPR=0.665, FPR=0.379, AUC=0.643
  speed: caught 15/40 (37.50%) rssi:
  caught 95/140 (67.86%) identity:
  caught 99/120 (82.50%)

=== Layer-3: Fusion ===
TPR=0.800, FPR=0.530, AUC=0.712
  speed: caught 31/40 (77.50%) rssi:
  caught 115/140 (82.14%) identity:
  caught 118/120 (98.33%)

=== No-Defense (reference) ===
TPR=0.000, FPR=0.000, AUC=0.500
```

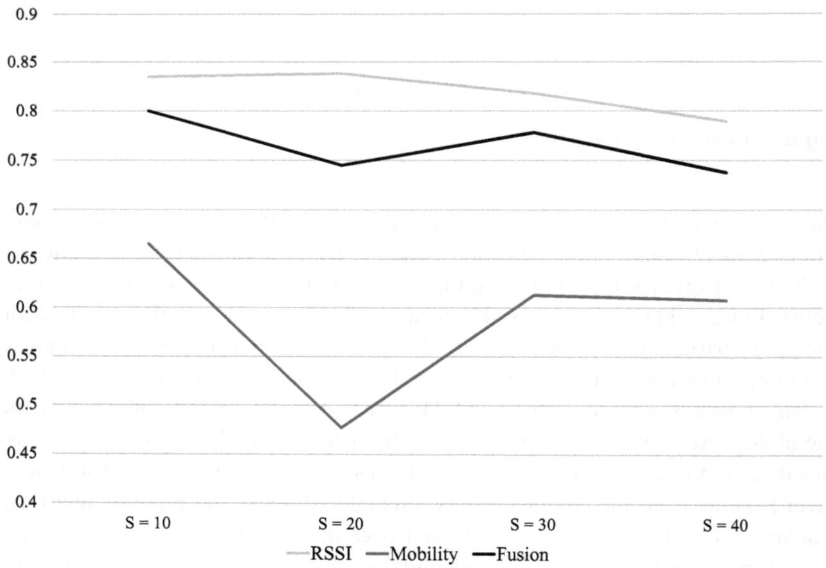

Fig. 6.2 Comparison of TPR for different S-values

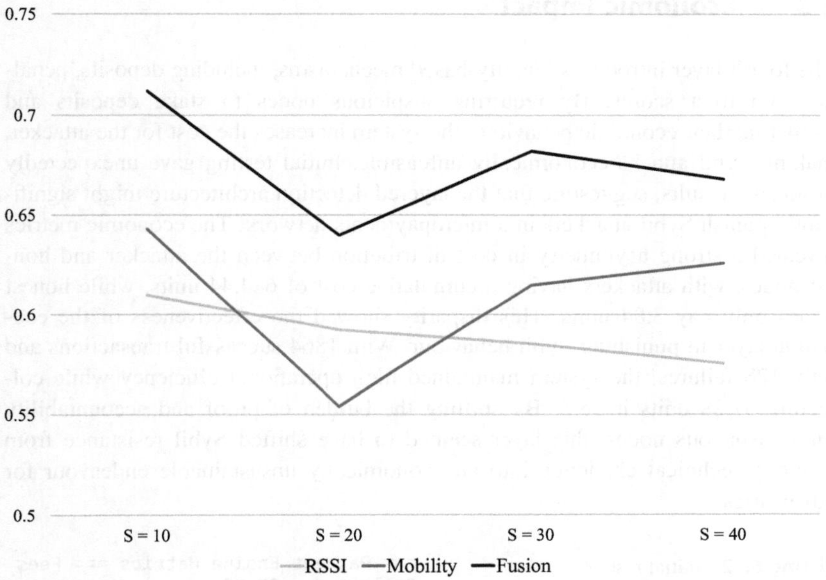

Fig. 6.3 Comparison of AUC for different S-values

Listing 6.11 S = 40

```
=== Layer-1: RSSI ===
TPR=0.830, FPR=0.592, AUC=0.619 speed:
  caught 229/260 (88.08%) rssi: caught
  404/460 (87.83%) identity: caught
  492/500 (98.40%)

=== Layer-2: Mobility ===
TPR=0.646, FPR=0.414, AUC=0.616 speed:
  caught 124/260 (47.69%) rssi: caught
  319/460 (69.35%) identity: caught
  393/500 (78.60%)

=== Layer-3: Fusion ===
TPR=0.794, FPR=0.511, AUC=0.714 speed:
  caught 221/260 (85.00%) rssi: caught
  393/460 (85.43%) identity: caught
  492/500 (98.40%)

=== No-Defense (reference) ===
TPR=0.000, FPR=0.000, AUC=0.500
```

6.3 Economic Impact

The fourth layer introduces identity-based mechanisms, including deposits, penalties and trust scores. By requiring suspicious nodes to stake deposits and validating their economic behaviour, the system increases the cost for the attacker, making Sybil attacks economically unfeasible. Initial testing gave unexpectedly promising results, suggesting that the layered detection architecture might significantly punish Sybil attackers in a micropayments network. The economic metrics revealed a strong asymmetry in cost distribution between the attacker and honest nodes, with attackers having a cumulative cost of 684.44 units, while honest nodes only pay 3.84 units. This disparity showed the effectiveness of the economic layer in punishing Sybil behaviour. With 1864 successful transactions and only 128 failures, the system maintained high operational efficiency while collecting 37.28 units in fees. By shifting the burden of proof and accountability onto suspicious nodes, this layer seemed to have shifted Sybil resistance from a purely technical challenge into an economically unsustainable endeavour for adversaries.

Listing 6.12 Initial results

```
=== Payment Engine Metrics === Fees
Collected : 37.28
Tx Success       : 1864
Failed Tx        : 128
Attacker Cost : 684.44
Honest Cost      : 3.84
```

However, upon further experimentation and attempts to replicate these outcomes, the results proved inconsistent and ultimately irreproducible. Despite using the same configurations and datasets, subsequent runs failed to match the earlier performance, raising questions about the reliability of the initial findings and the final, reproducible results are notably weaker. Stability of the payments network dropped significantly and the system struggled to actually punish sybil nodes while maintaining the capability to do transactions. These outcomes, while disappointing in terms of raw performance, offer valuable insights into the fragility of the micropayments when used in the context of IT security. They underscore the importance of robust testing, reproducibility, and transparency in evaluating security architectures.

Rather than dismissing the early results as anomalies, this thesis treats them as a signal to investigate in the future what conditions may have temporarily aligned to produce them and why these conditions failed to hold. The contrast between initial and final results highlights the volatility of performance in adversarial settings and points to key areas for future refinement.

Listing 6.13 N = 100

```
=== Payment Engine Metrics === Fees
Collected : 24.10
Tx Success       : 830
Failed Tx        : 570
Attacker Cost : 12.80
Honest Cost      : 11.30
```

These results do change with the number of Sybil and honest agents. The false positives additionally make the cost for honest nodes higher and due to the way the simulation is coded, it is unclear, what agents are causing the failed transactions.

Listing 6.14 N = 500

```
=== Payment Engine Metrics === Fees
Collected : 73.02
Tx Success       : 2335
Failed Tx        : 665
Attacker Cost : 10.80
Honest Cost      : 62.22
```

As there are more agents, the honest nodes pay is higher, mostly due to the fact that there are 10 times more honest agents than Sybil attackers. A network with many Sybil nodes compared to honest nodes leads to a better Honest to Attacker cost ratio, due to the many spamming attackers, the failed transactions also rise.

Listing 6.15 N = 100, S = 40

```
=== Payment Engine Metrics === Fees
Collected : 68.62
Tx Success       : 2406
Failed Tx        : 1994
Attacker Cost : 57.42
Honest Cost      : 11.20
```

7 Discussion

The layered architecture presented in this paper was designed with four core objectives in mind. The objectives being improving detection accuracy, preserving payment viability under attack, introducing economic deterrence and ensuring feasibility for deployment in constrained environments. Each of these goals reflects one of the challenges existing in decentralized networks, especially the ones vulnerable to Sybil attacks, where it is even more harmful to have multiple falsely created identities to subvert consensus or gain malicious benefits. Despite the ambitious design, the experimental results obtained during the evaluation phase were not as overwhelmingly positive as those reported in prior literature. This discrepancy can be attributed to several factors, most notably the imperfect recreation of the target environment within the simulation framework used in this thesis. Many of the detection approaches employed in the architecture have demonstrated high efficacy in their original, assumed contexts but when recreated into the simulation environment of this study, their performance was less consistent. This divergence may stem from inaccuracies in implementation, environmental noise and differences in system setup that were not fully accounted for during replication.

The experimental results demonstrate that the proposed system is capable of identifying Sybil nodes with a reasonable degree of accuracy. While not flawless, the detection mechanisms consistently distinguished malicious actors from honest participants across multiple scenarios. The integration of these diverse approaches within a unified framework gave promising outcomes, suggesting that meaningful synergies can be created when multiple detection strategies are layered and

K. A. Stiller, *Securing Peer-to-Peer Identities in IoT Systems Using Blockchain and Multi-Agent Systems with an Outlook on M2M Payment Applications*, BestMasters, https://doi.org/10.1007/978-3-658-51520-1_7

coordinated. These can be further explored in future work. One of the important aspects of the architecture is the interplay between its layers. The synergy between these layers played a big role in reducing the incidence of false positives—a critical metric in any detection system. In real-world deployments, where uninterrupted service and user trust are often more critical than perfect classification, minimizing false alarms is possibly more important than achieving perfect classification. The layered design, by balancing sensitivity and specificity across different detection modalities, offers a pragmatic solution to this challenge.

Each layer of the detection framework brings its own strengths and limitations to the table. Layer 1, which relies exclusively on RSSI ratios, consistently achieves high true positive rates, especially in scenarios with larger node populations. However, it is also more susceptible to false positives due to the inherent variability and noise in signal strength data. Layer 2, which analyses the mobility patterns, adopts a more conservative stance. Although its true positive rate is lower, it compensates with a reduced false positive rate, indicating a greater ability to avoid misclassifying honest nodes. On the other hand, it struggles to detect more difficult Sybil agents, especially those that mimic legitimate movement behaviours. Layer 3 serves as the integrative component, fusing the outputs of the first two layers through a weighted decision-making process. This layer strikes a balance between sensitivity and specificity and while its true positive rate occasionally falls below that of Layer 1, it consistently achieves a higher area under the ROC curve which is a strong indicator of overall detection accuracy (Fig. 7.1). But because it is based on the other two layers, its performance is sensitive to the biases of the underlying layers, especially when mobility-based detection disproportionately influences the final decision. This shows the importance of calibrating inter-layer influence to avoid amplifying systemic weaknesses.

Across all layers, identity-based Sybil nodes were detected with high reliability, often achieving accuracy rates over 0.97. This demonstrates the robustness of static identity verification mechanisms. In contrast, RSSI-based Sybils showed more variable detection rates, with Layer 1 performing best because of its direct reliance on signal strength analysis. Mobility-based Sybils were the biggest challenge, particularly in Layer 2, where detection rates dropped at lower node counts. This suggests that mobility patterns alone may not provide a sufficiently robust basis for Sybil identification, especially when legitimate nodes exhibit similar movement behaviours. To help in the interpretation of these results, ROC curves are plotted, showing the trade-off between true positive rates and false positive rates across different configurations showing a clear depiction of the performance

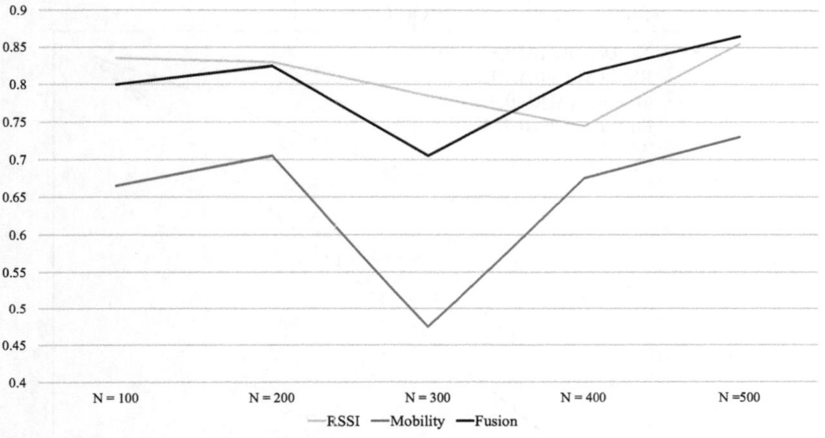

Fig. 7.1 Comparison of TPR across N

of the system and reinforce the conclusion that a layered approach with synergies to one that could balance precision, efficiency and adaptability enough in the future of machine-to-machine payments (Fig. 7.2).

Besides the detection, requiring nodes to place deposits and enforcing penalties for malicious behaviour, the system discourages malicious behaviour without relying solely on technical detection. However, this introduces a trade-off with higher deposit thresholds, while effective against attackers, may exclude low-resource nodes from participation, thereby compromising the inclusivity of the network. This tension between security and accessibility is a recurring theme in decentralized system design and must be carefully managed based on the specific deployment context. While the early detection layer aims to fight this, it would need to be more accurate to really reduce the costs for honest participants. That is why the identity ledger is also there for the redemption of falsely flagged nodes.

7.1 Contribution

From a Design Science Research perspective, the proposed system contributes insight rather than perfection. While the payment mechanism exhibited limitations under attack, highlighting areas for future refinement, the layered detection architecture demonstrated promising results in identifying Sybil nodes across diverse

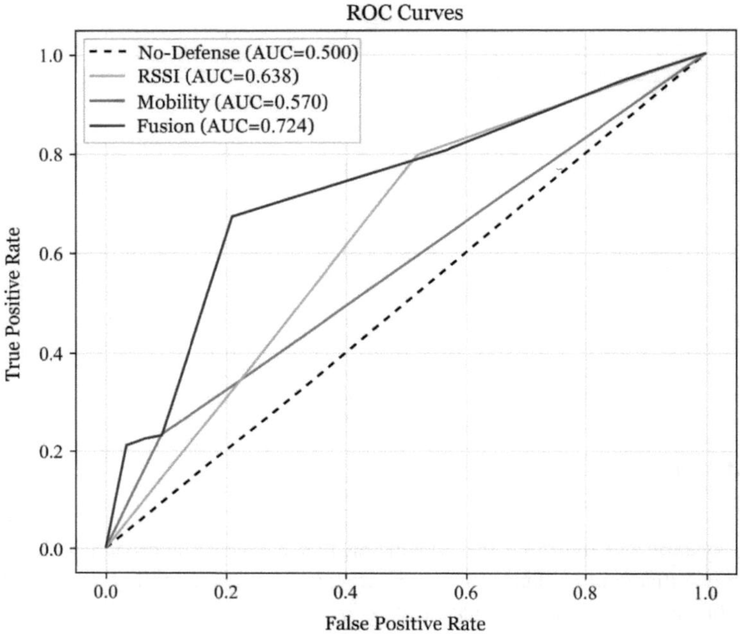

Fig. 7.2 Comparison of ROC curves

scenarios. Its contribution lies in revealing how different approaches and algorithms, when coordinated, can complement each other to reduce false positives and improve overall robustness.

The framework offers insight through its grounding in prior models and reproducible experimentation, and novelty through its hybrid integration of multi-agent simulation and blockchain-based economic deterrence and trust. Although the individual layers showed varying performance, their connection gave valuable design principles for balancing sensitivity and specificity in adversarial environments. This layered approach, while not yet optimal, provides a foundation for future systems that aim to maintain operational integrity and trust in machine-to-machine payment networks, even when under imperfect conditions.

7.2 Limitations

While the simulation environment aims to capture realistic network dynamics, certain abstractions were necessary to ensure tractability. While the configuration parameters allow for an in depth analysis of all situations, the study does not exhaustively explore parameter tuning for all detection thresholds, resulting in the findings acting more as a proof-of-concept rather than a real world example. In addition, the study is bounded by practical computational and timely constraints. The current implementation was executed on a single laptop system using Python, which naturally constrained the scale of experimentation. This choice ensured manageable run times and interpretability of results, but also means that certain performance bottlenecks or adversarial strategies that are only shown at extreme scale remain unexplored.

Recreating existing approaches from related literature also posed challenges. Many referenced papers lacked openly accessible code, relying instead on high level descriptions and without an openly accessible code from the used papers, basing implementation only on descriptions, pseudocode and mathematical equations, a perfect recreation of the featured approaches is very difficult and as there can be differences in implementation, leading to different results. With the time constraint of the thesis writing period, extensive testing for the perfect accuracy of the different approaches is limited and therefore the results of this simulation are meant to be seen as a proof of concept, not a completely accurate recreation and evaluation of the approaches used and not a perfect representation of a real world scenario. The approaches used were used for the base logic of their detection and the results they achieved in this paper's simulation are not a reflection of their success. Additionally, the current implementation has been tested on networks ranging with a very limited number of nodes, which, while sufficient for proof-of-concept, do not reflect the scale of real-world deployments involving millions of devices.

The simulator also uses simplified models for mobility and the ledger, which do not capture the full complexity of real-world behaviour. Additionally, hardware specific attacks such as RF fingerprinting and side-channel analysis are not explicitly modelled, limiting the system's ability to detect certain classes of sophisticated threats. These limitations point to clear directions for future work. Scaling the simulation, incorporating more realistic models and exploring hybrid defences that combine software and hardware-level detection will be important for advancing the system from prototype to production. Additionally, due to the ambitious scope of the initial research plan and the natural time constraints of the thesis writing period, several promising avenues could not be explored in full. These include deeper integration of related work, more fine-tuning of fusion weights between layers and extended simulations across broader network topologies. Nevertheless, the current study lays a strong foundation for future research. The insights gained—both from successes and shortcomings offer guidance for refining detection strategies, calibrating combined layer influence and designing systems that are not only accurate but also resilient and scalable.

7.2.1 Future Work

Building on the insights and limitations discussed, several promising directions are there for future research. One direction involves exploring ScatterID (Huang et al., 2019), the hardware-level fingerprinting technique that has demonstrated exceptional accuracy in Sybil detection. While this thesis focuses on software based methods for broader applicability and ease of deployment, benchmarking against ScatterID could highlight the main trade-offs between precision and scalability. Exploring how these hardware-based approaches perform in resource constrained IoT environments and whether hybrid models could combine their strengths with lightweight software detection—would be a valuable extension of this work.

The RSSI detection layer currently implements the interval check described in the literature giving a binary decision focused on nodes inside the interval, which would be classified as normal, or outside nodes, classified as Sybils. The same interval equation can also be used to derive a continuous confidence score by measuring the distance of η from the interval boundaries as opposed to the currently implemented biased weights calculation which led to shortcomings whenever the more favoured approach had difficulties. Such scores would enable more nuanced fusion with other detectors and adaptive weighting. Due to time constraints, this work retains the binary decision, but incorporating confidence levels is a promising direction for future work. Generally a better way to fight the high false positives while maintaining true positives would be very important, especially when further exploring the Sybil-punishing ledger mechanism. With a strong detection layer, the approach could lead to a economically scalable micropayment solution, off-loading the cost to attackers.

Other than detection logic, architectural enhancements could strengthen the system. A proof-of-location mechanism, adapted from VANET tolling schemes (Azam et al.,2022), could use roadside-unit-like beacons to issue location puzzles, verified pseudonymously via smart contracts, for payments requiring physical presence. This would add a physical presence requirement to certain transactions, increasing resistance to remote Sybil attacks. As a non-real-time diagnostic, the system could also perform offline Sybil pattern analysis on transaction graphs, using temporal and topological features to verify whether simulated attackers produce detectable subgraph patterns.

Another important direction for future work would be to enhance system resilience in real-world IoT environments. Especially in regards to supporting the M2M payments in such dynamic conditions, off-chain micropayment channels modelled after the Lightning Network (Robert, Kubler & Ghatpande, 2020) offer a promising solution. These channels enable frequent, low-latency transactions without incurring significant on-chain fees, making them well-suited for M2M interactions. Future evaluations could expand more on system-level metrics to assess operational efficiency and Sybil resistance. Key measurements include CPU usage and computation time per agent step and energy consumption approximated by transmission counts and trust-based routing load. Resilience can be further studied through controlled network partitions and churn events, analysing service continuity and the impact of revocation lag on performance.

Lastly, the broader theme that emerges is the importance of adaptive system configurations. Depending on operational needs, systems may need to prioritize speed, robustness or interpretability. Designing architectures that can dynamically tune these trade-offs through confidence aware fusion strategies or modular detection pipelines might still be important to making Sybil detection both scalable and resilient in M2M networks.

8 Conclusion

This thesis aimed to explore Sybil attack detection in Machine-to-Machine payment systems through a layered architectural approach using Multi-Agent Systems and Blockchain. While the results did not show outstanding performance, they revealed important insights into the dynamics of detection strategies, the balance between precision and scalability and the challenges of real-world applicability. The layered design of this approach, even though imperfect, showed that combining different detection approaches can reduce false positives and offer a more balanced detection framework, especially in environments where multiple types of attackers might be and even honest agents might behave unusual.

The experimental outcomes served as a proof-of-concept for how architectural synergy can be leveraged to detect and punish Sybil attackers. The limitations encountered, ranging from constrained simulation scale and simplified models, to the difficulty of replicating prior work without open-source implementations, highlighted both the complexity of the problem space and the need for more robust and feasible solutions. The shortcomings themselves proved to be insightful and instructive as they pointed to areas where future systems could improve like the refinement of fusion weights by incorporating actual confidence scores, adapting to intermittent connectivity and integrating hardware-level detection. These gaps are not failures but opportunities to deepen understanding and build stronger systems.

In the end, this thesis offers insight and a structured foundation instead of solving Sybil detection in its entirety. It gives a set of architectural principles and a reflection on what works, what does not work and what could work, being a step forward instead of the final answer.

K. A. Stiller, *Securing Peer-to-Peer Identities in IoT Systems Using Blockchain and Multi-Agent Systems with an Outlook on M2M Payment Applications*, BestMasters, https://doi.org/10.1007/978-3-658-51520-1_8

Bibliography

Abdelatif, H., Abdelhakim, S. H., & Mustapha, S. (2021). A tractable probabilistic approach to analyze Sybil attacks in sharding-based blockchain protocols. Retrieved from https://doi.org/10.48550/arXiv.2104.07215

Ahmed, D. E. M., & Khalifa, O. O. (2017). An overview of MANETs: applications, characteristics, challenges and recent issues. Retrieved from https://www.ijeat.org/portfolio-item/D4927046417

Afanasyev, I., Kolotov, A., Rezin, R., Danilov, K., Kashevnik, A., & Jotsov, V. (2019). Blockchain Solutions for Multi-Agent Robotic Systems: Related Work and Open Questions. https://doi.org/10.48550/arXiv.1903.11041

Afzaal, H., Imran, M., & Janjua, M. U. (2023). Formal verification of fraud-resilience in a crowdsourcing consensus protocol. Retrieved from https://doi.org/10.1016/j.cose.2023.103290

Akhtar, F., Rehmani, M. H., Reisslein, M. (2016). White space: Definitional perspectives and their role in exploiting spectrum opportunities. Retrieved from https://doi.org/10.1016/j.telpol.2016.01.003

Al-Fuqaha, A., Guizani, M., Mohammadi, M., Aledhari, M., & Ayyash, M. (2015). Internet of Things: A Survey on Enabling Technologies, Protocols and Applications. In: IEEE Communications Surveys & Tutorials, vol. 17, no. 4, pp. 2347–2376. Retrieved from https://doi.org/10.1109/COMST.2015.2444095

Arshad, A., Hanapi, Z. M., Subramaniam, S., & Latip, R. (2021). A survey of Sybil attack countermeasures in IoT-based wireless sensor networks. Retrieved from https://peerj.com/articles/cs-673/

Ashton, K. (2009). That 'Internet of Things' Thing: In the Real World Things Matter More than Ideas. Retrieved from https://www.rfidjournal.com/expert-views/that-internet-of-things-thing/73881/

Atzori, L., Iera, A., & Morabito, G. (2010). The Internet of Things: A suvery. Retrieved from https://doi.org/10.1016/j.comnet.2010.05.010

Bochem, A., & Leiding, B. (2021). Rechained: Sybil-resistant distributed identities for the Internet of Things and mobile ad hoc networks. Retrieved from https://doi.org/10.3390/s21093257

K. A. Stiller, *Securing Peer-to-Peer Identities in IoT Systems Using Blockchain and Multi-Agent Systems with an Outlook on M2M Payment Applications*, BestMasters, https://doi.org/10.1007/978-3-658-51520-1

Commerzbank AG. (2019, August 8). Commerzbank testet erstmals Blockchainbasierte Maschine-zu-Maschine-Zahlung. Retrieved from https://www.commerzbank.de/konzern/newsroom/pressemitteilungen/bbmzm-zahlung.html

Dayyani, A., & Abbaspour, M. (2024). SybilPSIoT: Preventing Sybil attacks in signed social internet of things based on web of trust and smart contract. Retrieved from https://doi.org/10.1049/cmu2.12734

De Campos, M. G., Chanel, C. P. C., Chauffaut, C., & Lacan, J. (2021). Towards a Blockchain-Based Multi-UAV Surveillance System. Retrieved from https://doi.org/10.3389/frobt.2021.557692

Dempsey, K., Chawla, N. S., Johnson, A., Johnston, R., Jones, A. C., Orebaugh, A., Scholl, M., & Stine, K. (2011). Special Publication 800-137. Retrieved from https://doi.org/10.6028/NIST.SP.800-137

Dong, X., Wu, Y., Xu, M., & Zheng, N. (2022). Resilient consensus for multi-agent systems in the presence of Sybil attacks. Retrieved from https://doi.org/10.3390/electronics11050800

Dorri, A., Kanhere, S. S., & Jurdak, R. (2018). Multi-Agent Systems: A Survey. Retrieved from https://doi.org/10.1109/ACCESS.2018.2831228

Garzon, S. R., Yildiz, H., & Küpper, A. (2022). Towards Decentralized Identity Management in Multi-stakeholder 6G Networks. Retrieved from https://doi.org/10.1109/6GNet54646.2022.9830163

Ghiro, L., Restuccia, F., D'Oro, S., Basagni, S., Melodia, T., & Maccari, L. (2021). A Blockchain Definition to Clarify its Role for the Internet of Things. Retrieved from https://doi.org/10.1109/MedComNet52149.2021.9501280

Hevner, A. R., March, S. T., Park, J. & Ram, S., (2004). Design Science in Information Systems Research. Retrieved from https://doi.org/10.2307/25148625

Huang, Y., Wang, W., Wang, Y., Jiang, T., & Zhang, Q. (2019). Lightweight Sybil-resilient multi-robot networks by multipath manipulation. Retrieved from https://doi.org/10.48550/arXiv.1912.04613

Hussain, M. Z., Hanapi, Z. M., Abdullah, A., Hussin, M., & Ninggal, M. I. H. (2024). An efficient secure and energy resilient trust-based system for detection and mitigation of Sybil attack detection (SAN). Retrieved from https://peerj.com/articles/cs-2231/

Igor, Z., Maslennikov, O., Lebedev, I., Ometov, A., & Andreev, S., (2016). Dynamic Trust Management Framework for Robotic Multi-Agent Systems. Retrieved from https://doi.org/10.1007/978-3-319-46301-8_28

Jamil, F., Cheikhrouhou, O., Jamil, H., Koubaa, A., Derhab, A., Ferrag, M. A. (2021). PetroBlock: A Blockchain-Based Payment Mechanism for Fueling Smart Vehicles. Retrieved from https://doi.org/10.3390/app11073055

Jamshidi, M., Zangeneh, E., Esnaashari, M., & Meybodi, M. R. (2017). A lightweight algorithm for detecting mobile Sybil nodes in mobile wireless sensor networks. In: Computers & Electrical Engineering, 64, 220–232. Retrieved from https://doi.org/10.1016/j.compeleceng.2016.12.011

Jan, M. A., Nanda, P., He, X., & Liu, R. P. (2016). A Sybil attack detection scheme for a forest wildfire monitoring application. Retrieved from https://doi.org/10.1016/j.future.2016.05.034

Keramat, F., Queralta, J. P., & Westerlund, T. (2023). Partition-tolerant and Byzantine-tolerant decision making for distributed robotic systems with IOTA and ROS2. In: IEEE

Internet of Things Journal, vol. 10, no. 14, pp. 12985–12998. Retrieved from https://doi.org/10.1109/JIOT.2023.3257984

Khan, M. A., & Salah, K. (2018). IoT security: Review, blockchain solutions, and open challenges. Retrieved from https://doi.org/10.1016/j.future.2017.11.022

Khatri, N., Lee, S., & Nam, S. Y. (2024). Sybil attack-resistant blockchain-based proof-of-location mechanism with privacy protection in VANET. Retrieved from https://doi.org/10.3390/s24248140

Liang, C., Shanmugam, B., Azam, S., Karim, A., Islam, A., Zamani, M., Kavianpour, S., & Idris, N. B. (2020). Intrusion Detection System for the Internet of Things Based on Blockchain and Multi-Agent Systems. Retrieved from https://doi.org/10.3390/electronics9071120

Liu, Q., Huang, Q., Fan, F., Wu, H., & Tang, X. (2025). Detecting Sybil addresses in blockchain airdrops: A subgraph-based feature propagation and fusion approach. Retrieved from https://doi.org/10.48550/arXiv.2505.09313

Madakam, S., Ranaswany, R., & Tripathi, S. (2015). Internet of Things (IoT): A Literature Review. Retrieved from https://doi.org/10.4236/jcc.2015.35021

Mastercard. (2021). How IoT will shape the future of payments. Retrieved from https://www.mastercard.com/news/media/wddjfrhn/how-iot-will-shape-the-future-of-payments.pdf

Mercan, S., & Akkaya, K. (2021). Building Next Generation IoT Infrastructure for Enabling M2M Crypto Economy. Retrieved from https://www.ronpub.com/ojiot/OJIOT_2021v7i1n11_Mercan.html

Mercan, S., Kurt, A., Akkaya, K., & Erdin, E. (2022). Cryptocurrency solutions to enable micropayments in consumer IoT. Retrieved from https://doi.org/10.1109/MCE.2021.3060720

Mourouzis, T., & Markou, N. (2022). Blockchains, DLTs and the future of payments. In N. Vadgama, J. Xu, & P. Tasca (Eds.), Enabling the Internet of Value. Retrieved from https://doi.org/10.1007/978-3-030-78184-2_3

Nakamoto, S. (2008). Bitcoin: A Peer-to-Peer Electronic Cash System. Retrieved from https://bitcoin.org/bitcoin.pdf

Netto, V. H. M., Cholez, T., & Ignat, C. L. (2025). Active Sybil attack and efficient defense strategy in IPFS DHT. Retrieved from https://doi.org/10.48550/arXiv.2505.01139

Otte, P., de Vos, M., & Pouwelse, J. (2020). TrustChain: A Sybil-resistant scalable blockchain. In: Future Generation Computer Systems, 107, 770–780. Retrieved from https://doi.org/10.1016/j.future.2017.08.048

Peffers, K., Tuunanen, T., Rothenberger, M. A., & Chatterjee, S., (2007). A Design Science Research Methodology for Information Systems Research. In: Journal of Management Information Systems, 24(3), 45–77. Retrieved from https://doi.org/10.2753/MIS0742-1222240302

Pocher, N., & Zichichi, M. (2022). Towards CBDC-based machine-to-machine payments in consumer IoT. Retrieved from https://doi.org/10.1145/3477314.3507078

Pradhan, D., & Tun, H. M. (2022). Security Challenges: M2M Communication in IoT. Retrieved from https://doi.org/10.36548/jeea.2022.3.006

Rajadurai, H., & Gandhi, U. D. (2019). Fuzzy based collaborative verification system for Sybil attack detection in MANET. Retrieved from https://link.springer.com/article/10.1007/s11277-019-06836-7

Reed, D., Sporny, M., Longley, D., Allen, C., Grant, R., & Sabadello, M. (2022). Decentralized identifiers (DIDs) v1.0. Retrieved from https://www.w3.org/TR/did-core/

Robert, J., Kubler, S., & Ghatpande, S. (2020). Enhanced Lightning Network (off-chain)-based micropayment in IoT ecosystems. Retrieved from https://doi.org/10.1016/j.future.2020.05.033

Rojek, I., Kotlarz, P., Dorozynski, J., & Mikolajewski, D. (2024). Sixthgeneration (6G) networks for improved machine-to-machine (M2M) communication. Retrieved from https://doi.org/10.3390/electronics13101832

Saldana, D., Prorok, A., Sundaram, S., Campos, M. F. M., & Kumar, V. (2017). Resilient Consensus for Time-Varying Networks of Dynamic Agents. Retrieved from https://doi.org/10.23919/ACC.2017.7962962

SNS Insider. (2025, February). Machine-to-machine (M2M) market size, share & segment by technology, component, application, and global forecast 2024–2032. Retrieved from https://www.snsinsider.com/reports/machine-to-machine-market-5622

Serena, L., D'Angelo, G., & Ferretti, S. (2021). Security analysis of distributed ledgers and blockchains through agent-based simulation. Retrieved from https://doi.org/10.48550/arXiv.2109.08358

Shamshirband, S., Anuar, N. B., Kiah, M. L. M., & Patel, A. (2013). An appraisal and design of a multi-agent system based cooperative wireless intrusion detection computational intelligence technique. Retrieved from https://doi.org/10.1016/j.engappai.2013.04.010

Stokkink, Q., Ileri, C. U., Epema, D., & Pouwelse, J. (2023). Web3 Sybil avoidance using network latency. Retrieved from https://doi.org/10.1016/j.comnet.2023.109701

Szabo, N. (1997). Formalizing and Securing Relationships on Public Networks. Retrieved from https://firstmonday.org/ojs/index.php/fm/article/download/548/469

Strobel, V., Ferrer, E. C., & Dorigo, M. (2020). Blockchain Technology Secures Robot Swarms: A Comparison of Consensus Protocols and Their Resilience to Byzantine Robots. Retrieved from https://doi.org/10.3389/frobt.2020.00054

Tuunanen, T., Winter, R., & vom Brocke, J. (2024). Dealing with complexity in design science research: A methodology using design echelons. Retrieved from https://doi.org/10.25300/MISQ/2023/16700

Venable, J., Pries-Heje, J. & Baskerville, R., (2016) FEDS: a Framework for Evaluation in Design Science Research. European Journal of Information Systems, 25(1), 77–89. Retrieved from https://doi.org/10.1057/ejis.2014.36

Watson, D., Piette, M., Sezgen, O., Motegi, N., & ten Hope, L. (2004). Machine-to-machine (M2M) technology in demand responsive commercial buildings. Retrieved from https://escholarship.org/uc/item/3286r367

Xu, Z., Salehi Shahraki, A., & Chilamkurti, N. (2024). A novel endorsement protocol to secure BFT-based consensus in permissionless blockchain. Retrieved from https://doi.org/10.1109/WCNC57260.2024.10570504

Yan, J., Jiang, T., Lin, L., Wu, Z., Ye, X., Tian, M., & Wang, Y. (2023). A novel Sybil attack detection scheme in mobile IoT based on collaborative edge computing. Retrieved from https://doi.org/10.1186/s13638-023-02233-8

Yang, Y., & Wang, J. (2008). Design Guidelines for Routing Metrics in Multihop Wireless Networks. Retrieved from https://doi.org/10.1109/INFOCOM.2008.222

Yang, Y., Wu, L., Yin, G., Li, L., & Zhao, H. (2017). A Survey on Security and Privacy Issues in Internet-of-Things. In: IEEE Internet of Things Journal, vol. 4, no. 5, pp. 1250–1258. Retrieved from https://doi.org/10.1109/JIOT.2017.2694844

Yaacoub, J. A., Noura, H. N., Salman, O., & Chehab, A. (2021). Robotics cyber security: vulnerabilities, attacks, countermeasures, and recommendations. Retrieved from https://doi.org/10.1007/s10207-021-00545-8

Yu, H., Kaminsky, M., Gibbons, P. B., & Flaxman, A. (2006). SybilGuard: defending against sybil attacks via social networks. Retrieved from https://doi.org/10.1145/1159913.1159945

Zhang, K., Liang, X., Lu, R., & Shen, X. (2014). Sybil Attacks and Their Defenses in the Internet of Things. Retrieved from https://doi.org/10.1109/JIOT.2014.2344013

MIX
Papier aus verantwortungsvollen Quellen
Paper from responsible sources
FSC® C105338

If you have any concerns about our products,
you can contact us on
ProductSafety@springernature.com

In case Publisher is established outside the EU,
the EU authorized representative is:
Springer Nature Customer Service Center GmbH
Europaplatz 3, 69115 Heidelberg, Germany

Printed by Libri Plureos GmbH
in Hamburg, Germany